I0007014

Python - A Beginner's Guide

Take your first step towards a career in software development with this introduction to python, one of the most in-demand programming language. Designed for beginners, this python tutorial book will provide you with a basic foundation in syntax, which is the first step towards becoming a successful python developer. You'll learn how computers make decisions and how python keeps track of information through variables and data types. You'll learn to create conditional statements, functions, and loops to process information and solve coding problems. These are fundamental programming skills, and mastering them is a must for all aspiring programmers.

What you will learn in this book:

•Overview
•Environment Setup
•Basic Syntax
•Variable Types
•Basic Operators
•Decision making
•Loops
•Numbers
•Strings
•Lists
•Tuples
•Dictionary
•Date & Time
•Functions
•Modules
•Files I/O
•Exceptions Handling

- Object Oriented Programming
- CGI Programming
- MySQL Database
- Network Programming
- SMPT
- Multithreaded Programming
- XML Processing
- GUI Programming

Table of Contents

Python - A Beginner's Guide

Python Tutorial for Beginners

Python is a general-purpose, open source computer programming language. It is optimized for software quality, developer productivity, program portability, and component integration. Python is used by at least hundreds of thousands of developers around the world in areas such as Internet scripting, systems programming, user interfaces, product customization, numeric programming, and more. It is generally considered to be among the top four or five most widely-used programming languages in the world today.

As a popular language focused on shrinking development time, Python is deployed in a wide variety of products and roles. Counted among its current user base are Google, YouTube, Industrial Light & Magic, ESRI, the BitTorrent file sharing system, NASA's Jet Propulsion Lab, the game Eve Online, and the National Weather Service. Python's application domains range from system administration, website development, cell phone scripting, and education to hardware testing, investment analysis, computer games, and spacecraft control. Among other things, Python sports a remarkably simple, readable, and maintainable syntax; integration with external components coded in other languages; a multiparadigm design, with OOP, functional, and modular structures; and a vast collection of precoded interfaces and utilities. Its tool set makes it a flexible and agile language, ideal for both quick tactical tasks as well as longer-range strategic application development efforts. Although it is a general-purpose language,

Python is often called a scripting language because it makes it easy to utilize and direct other software components. Perhaps Python's best asset, though, is simply that it makes software development more rapid and enjoyable. There is a class of people for whom programming is an end in itself. They enjoy the challenge. They write software for the pure pleasure of doing so and often view commercial or career reward as secondary consequence. This is the class that largely invented the Internet, open source, and Python. This is also the class that has historically been a primary audience for this book. As they've often relayed, with a tool like Python, programming can be just plain fun. To truly understand how, read on; though something of a side effect, much of this book serves as a demonstration of Python's ideals in action in real-world code. As we'll see, especially when combined with toolkits for GUIs, websites, systems programming, and so on, Python serves as enabling technology.

To whom this tutorial is designed for:

This book is a tutorial introduction to using Python in common application domains and tasks. It teaches how to apply Python for system administration, GUIs, and the Web, and explores its roles in networking, databases, frontend scripting layers, text processing, and more. Although the Python language is used along the way, this book's focus is on language fundamentals.

Prerequisites:

Before proceeding with this tutorial you should have at least basic understanding of computer programming, Internet, Database, and MySQL etc is very helpful.

Python – Introduction

Python is a high-level, interpreted, interactive and object-oriented scripting language. Python is designed to be highly readable. It uses English keywords frequently where as other languages use punctuation, and it has fewer syntactical constructions than other languages.

- **Python is Interpreted** − Python is processed at runtime by the interpreter. You do not need to compile your program before executing it. This is similar to PERL and PHP.

- **Python is Interactive** − You can actually sit at a Python prompt and interact with the interpreter directly to write your programs.

- **Python is Object-Oriented** − Python supports Object-Oriented style or technique of programming that encapsulates code within objects.

- **Python is a Beginner's Language** − Python is a great language for the beginner-level programmers and supports the development of a wide range of applications from simple text processing to WWW browsers to games.

History of Python:

Python was developed by Guido van Rossum in the late eighties and early nineties at the National Research Institute for Mathematics and Computer Science in the Netherlands.

Python is derived from many other languages, including ABC, Modula-3, C, C++, Algol-68, SmallTalk, and Unix shell and other scripting languages.

Python is copyrighted. Like Perl, Python source code is now available under the GNU General Public License (GPL).

Python is now maintained by a core development team at the institute, although Guido van Rossum still holds a vital role in directing its progress.

Python Features:

Python's feature includes:

- **Easy-to-learn** – Python has few keywords, simple structure, and a clearly defined syntax. This allows the student to pick up the language quickly.

- **Easy-to-read** – Python code is more clearly defined and visible to the eyes.

- **Easy-to-maintain** – Python's source code is fairly easy-to-maintain.

- **A broad standard library** – Python's bulk of the library is very portable and cross-platform compatible on UNIX, Windows, and Macintosh.

- **Interactive Mode** – Python has support for an interactive mode which allows interactive testing and debugging of snippets of code.

- **Portable** – Python can run on a wide variety of hardware platforms and has the same interface on all platforms.

- **Extendable** – You can add low-level modules to the Python interpreter. These modules enable programmers to add to or customize their tools to be more efficient.

- **Databases** – Python provides interfaces to all major commercial databases.

- **GUI Programming** – Python supports GUI applications that can be created and ported to many system calls, libraries and windows systems, such as Windows MFC, Macintosh, and the X Window system of Unix.

- **Scalable** – Python provides a better structure and support for large programs than shell scripting.

Apart from the above-mentioned features, Python has a big list of good features, few are listed below −

- It supports functional and structured programming methods as well as OOP.

- It can be used as a scripting language or can be compiled to byte-code for building large applications.

- It provides very high-level dynamic data types and supports dynamic type checking.

- It supports automatic garbage collection.

- It can be easily integrated with C, C++, COM, ActiveX, CORBA, and Java.

Python - Environment Setup

Python is available on a wide variety of platforms including Linux and Mac OS X. Let's understand how to set up our Python environment.

Local Environment Setup:

Open a terminal window and type "python" to find out if it is already installed and which version is installed.

- Unix (Solaris, Linux, FreeBSD, AIX, HP/UX, SunOS, IRIX, etc.)
- Win 9x/NT/2000
- Macintosh (Intel, PPC, 68K)
- OS/2
- DOS (multiple versions)
- PalmOS
- Nokia mobile phones
- Windows CE
- Acorn/RISC OS
- BeOS
- Amiga
- VMS/OpenVMS
- QNX
- VxWorks
- Psion

- Python has also been ported to the Java and .NET virtual machines

Getting Python:

The most up-to-date and current source code, binaries, documentation, news, etc., is available on the official website of Python https://www.python.org/

You can download Python documentation from https://www.python.org/doc/. The documentation is available in HTML, PDF, and PostScript formats.

Installing Python:

Python distribution is available for a wide variety of platforms. You need to download only the binary code applicable for your platform and install Python.

If the binary code for your platform is not available, you need a C compiler to compile the source code manually. Compiling the source code offers more flexibility in terms of choice of features that you require in your installation.

Here is a quick overview of installing Python on various platforms –

Unix and Linux Installation:

Here are the simple steps to install Python on Unix/Linux machine.

- Open a Web browser and go to https://www.python.org/downloads/.

- Follow the link to download zipped source code available for Unix/Linux.

- Download and extract files.

- Editing the *Modules/Setup* file if you want to customize some options.

- run ./configure script

- make

- make install

This installs Python at standard location */usr/local/bin* and its libraries at */usr/local/lib/pythonXX* where XX is the version of Python.

Windows Installation:

Here are the steps to install Python on Windows machine.

- Open a Web browser and go to https://www.python.org/downloads/.

- Follow the link for the Windows installer *python-XYZ.msi* file where XYZ is the version you need to install.

- To use this installer *python-XYZ.msi*, the Windows system must support Microsoft Installer 2.0. Save the installer file to your local machine and then run it to find out if your machine supports MSI.

- Run the downloaded file. This brings up the Python install wizard, which is really easy to use. Just accept the default settings, wait until the install is finished, and you are done.

Macintosh Installation:

Recent Macs come with Python installed, but it may be several years out of date. See http://www.python.org/download/mac/for instructions on getting the current version along with extra tools to support development on the Mac. For older Mac OS's before Mac OS X 10.3 (released in 2003), MacPython is available.

Jack Jansen maintains it and you can have full access to the entire documentation at his website – http://www.cwi.nl/~jack/macpython.html. You can find complete installation details for Mac OS installation.

Setting up PATH:

Programs and other executable files can be in many directories, so operating systems provide a search path that lists the directories that the OS searches for executables.

The path is stored in an environment variable, which is a named string maintained by the operating system. This variable contains information available to the command shell and other programs.

The **path** variable is named as PATH in Unix or Path in Windows (Unix is case sensitive; Windows is not).

In Mac OS, the installer handles the path details. To invoke the Python interpreter from any particular directory, you must add the Python directory to your path.

Setting path at Unix/Linux:

To add the Python directory to the path for a particular session in Unix –

- **In the csh shell** – type setenv PATH "$PATH:/usr/local/bin/python" and press Enter.

- **In the bash shell (Linux)** – type export PATH="$PATH:/usr/local/bin/python" and press Enter.

- **In the sh or ksh shell** – type PATH="$PATH:/usr/local/bin/python" and press Enter.

- **Note** – /usr/local/bin/python is the path of the Python directory

Setting path at Windows:

To add the Python directory to the path for a particular session in Windows −

At the command prompt − type path %path%;C:\Python and press Enter.

Note − C:\Python is the path of the Python directory

Python Environment Variables:

Here are important environment variables, which can be recognized by Python −

Sr.No.	Variable & Description
1	**PYTHONPATH** It has a role similar to PATH. This variable tells the Python interpreter where to locate the module files imported into a program. It should include the Python source library directory and the directories containing Python source code. PYTHONPATH is sometimes preset by the Python installer.
2	**PYTHONSTARTUP** It contains the path of an initialization file

	containing Python source code. It is executed every time you start the interpreter. It is named as .pythonrc.py in Unix and it contains commands that load utilities or modify PYTHONPATH.
3	**PYTHONCASEOK** It is used in Windows to instruct Python to find the first case-insensitive match in an import statement. Set this variable to any value to activate it.
4	**PYTHONHOME** It is an alternative module search path. It is usually embedded in the PYTHONSTARTUP or PYTHONPATH directories to make switching module libraries easy.

Running Python:

There are three different ways to start Python –

Interactive Interpreter:

You can start Python from Unix, DOS, or any other system that provides you a command-line interpreter or shell window.

Enter **python** the command line.

Start coding right away in the interactive interpreter.

```
$python # Unix/Linux
or
python% # Unix/Linux
or
C:> python # Windows/DOS
```

Here is the list of all the available command line options −

Sr.No.	Option & Description
1	**-d** It provides debug output.
2	**-O** It generates optimized bytecode (resulting in .pyo files).
3	**-S** Do not run import site to look for Python paths on startup.
4	**-v**

	verbose output (detailed trace on import statements).
5	**-X** disable class-based built-in exceptions (just use strings); obsolete starting with version 1.6.
6	**-c cmd** run Python script sent in as cmd string
7	**file** run Python script from given file

Script from the Command-line:

A Python script can be executed at command line by invoking the interpreter on your application, as in the following –

```
$python script.py # Unix/Linux

or

python% script.py # Unix/Linux
```

or

```
C: >python script.py # Windows/DOS
```

Note – Be sure the file permission mode allows execution.

Integrated Development Environment:

You can run Python from a Graphical User Interface (GUI) environment as well, if you have a GUI application on your system that supports Python.

- **Unix** – IDLE is the very first Unix IDE for Python.

- **Windows** – PythonWin is the first Windows interface for Python and is an IDE with a GUI.

- **Macintosh** – The Macintosh version of Python along with the IDLE IDE is available from the main website, downloadable as either MacBinary or BinHex'd files.

If you are not able to set up the environment properly, then you can take help from your system admin. Make sure the Python environment is properly set up and working perfectly fine.

Python - Basic Syntax

The Python language has many similarities to Perl, C, and Java. However, there are some definite differences between the languages.

First Python Program:

Let us execute programs in different modes of programming.

Interactive Mode Programming:

Invoking the interpreter without passing a script file as a parameter brings up the following prompt −

```
$ python

Python 2.4.3 (#1, Nov 11 2010, 13:34:43)

[GCC 4.1.2 20080704 (Red Hat 4.1.2-48)] on linux2

Type "help", "copyright", "credits" or "license" for more information.

>>>
```

Type the following text at the Python prompt and press the Enter −

```
>>> print "Hello, Python!"
```

If you are running new version of Python, then you would need to use print statement with parenthesis as in **print ("Hello, Python!");**. However in Python version 2.4.3, this produces the following result −

```
Hello, Python!
```

Script Mode Programming:

Invoking the interpreter with a script parameter begins execution of the script and continues until the script is finished. When the script is finished, the interpreter is no longer active.

Let us write a simple Python program in a script. Python files have extension **.py**. Type the following source code in a test.py file −

```
print "Hello, Python!"
```

We assume that you have Python interpreter set in PATH variable. Now, try to run this program as follows −

```
$ python test.py
```

This produces the following result −

```
Hello, Python!
```

Let us try another way to execute a Python script. Here is the modified test.py file −

```
#!/usr/bin/python

print "Hello, Python!"
```

We assume that you have Python interpreter available in /usr/bin directory. Now, try to run this program as follows –

```
$ chmod +x test.py    # This is to make file executable
$ ./test.py
```

This produces the following result –

```
Hello, Python!
```

Python Identifiers:

A Python identifier is a name used to identify a variable, function, class, module or other object. An identifier starts with a letter A to Z or a to z or an underscore (_) followed by zero or more letters, underscores and digits (0 to 9).

Python does not allow punctuation characters such as @, $, and % within identifiers. Python is a case sensitive programming   language. Thus, **Manpower** and **manpower** are   two   different identifiers in Python.

Here are naming conventions for Python identifiers –

- Class names start with an uppercase letter. All other identifiers start with a lowercase letter.

- Starting an identifier with a single leading underscore indicates that the identifier is private.

- Starting an identifier with two leading underscores indicates a strongly private identifier.

- If the identifier also ends with two trailing underscores, the identifier is a language-defined special name.

Reserved Words:

The following list shows the Python keywords. These are reserved words and you cannot use them as constant or variable or any other identifier names. All the Python keywords contain lowercase letters only.

and	exec	not
assert	finally	or
break	for	pass
class	from	print
continue	global	raise

dcf	if	return
del	import	try
elif	in	while
else	is	with
except	lambda	yield

Lines and Indentation:

Python provides no braces to indicate blocks of code for class and function definitions or flow control. Blocks of code are denoted by line indentation, which is rigidly enforced.

The number of spaces in the indentation is variable, but all statements within the block must be indented the same amount. For example –

```
if True:
   print "True"
else:
   print "False"
```

However, the following block generates an error –

```
if True:

print "Answer"

print "True"

else:

print "Answer"

print "False"
```

Thus, in Python all the continuous lines indented with same number of spaces would form a block. The following example has various statement blocks –

Note – Do not try to understand the logic at this point of time. Just make sure you understood various blocks even if they are without braces.

```
#!/usr/bin/python

import sys

try:
   # open file stream
   file = open(file_name, "w")
except IOError:
```

```
      print "There was an error writing to", file_name

      sys.exit()

print "Enter '", file_finish,

print "' When finished"

while file_text != file_finish:

   file_text = raw_input("Enter text: ")

   if file_text == file_finish:

      # close the file

      file.close

      break

   file.write(file_text)

   file.write("\n")

file.close()

file_name = raw_input("Enter filename: ")

if len(file_name) == 0:

   print "Next time please enter something"

   sys.exit()

try:

   file = open(file_name, "r")
```

```
except IOError:

  print "There was an error reading file"

  sys.exit()

file_text = file.read()

file.close()

print file_text
```

Multi-Line Statements:

Statements in Python typically end with a new line. Python does, however, allow the use of the line continuation character (\) to denote that the line should continue. For example −

```
total = item_one + \
    item_two + \
    item_three
```

Statements contained within the [], {}, or () brackets do not need to use the line continuation character. For example −

```
days = ['Monday', 'Tuesday', 'Wednesday',
    'Thursday', 'Friday']
```

Quotation in Python:

Python accepts single ('), double (") and triple (''' or """) quotes to denote string literals, as long as the same type of quote starts and ends the string.

The triple quotes are used to span the string across multiple lines. For example, all the following are legal –

```
word = 'word'
sentence = "This is a sentence."
paragraph = """This is a paragraph. It is
made up of multiple lines and sentences."""
```

Comments in Python:

A hash sign (#) that is not inside a string literal begins a comment. All characters after the # and up to the end of the physical line are part of the comment and the Python interpreter ignores them.

```
#!/usr/bin/python


# First comment

print "Hello, Python!" # second comment
```

This produces the following result –

```
Hello, Python!
```

You can type a comment on the same line after a statement or expression –

```
name = "Madisetti" # This is again comment
```

You can comment multiple lines as follows –

```
# This is a comment.
# This is a comment, too.
# This is a comment, too.
# I said that already.
```

Using Blank Lines:

A line containing only whitespace, possibly with a comment, is known as a blank line and Python totally ignores it.

In an interactive interpreter session, you must enter an empty physical line to terminate a multiline statement.

Waiting for the User:

The following line of the program displays the prompt, the statement saying "Press the enter key to exit", and waits for the user to take action –

```
#!/usr/bin/python
```

```
raw_input("\n\nPress the enter key to exit.")
```

Here, "\n\n" is used to create two new lines before displaying the actual line. Once the user presses the key, the program ends. This is a nice trick to keep a console window open until the user is done with an application.

Multiple Statements on a Single Line:

The semicolon (;) allows multiple statements on the single line given that neither statement starts a new code block. Here is a sample snip using the semicolon –

```
import sys; x = 'foo'; sys.stdout.write(x + '\n')
```

Multiple Statement Groups as Suites:

A group of individual statements, which make a single code block are called **suites** in Python. Compound or complex statements, such as if, while, def, and class require a header line and a suite.

Header lines begin the statement (with the keyword) and terminate with a colon (:) and are followed by one or more lines which make up the suite. For example –

```
if expression :
   suite
elif expression :
   suite
else :
   suite
```

Command Line Arguments:

Many programs can be run to provide you with some basic information about how they should be run. Python enables you to do this with -h −

$ python -h

usage: python [option] ... [-c cmd | -m mod | file | -] [arg] ...

Options and arguments (and corresponding environment variables):

-c cmd : program passed in as string (terminates option list)

-d   : debug output from parser (also PYTHONDEBUG=x)

-E   : ignore environment variables (such as PYTHONPATH)

-h   : print this help message and exit

[etc.]

You can also program your script in such a way that it should accept various options.

Python - Variable Types

Variables are nothing but reserved memory locations to store values. This means that when you create a variable you reserve some space in memory.

Based on the data type of a variable, the interpreter allocates memory and decides what can be stored in the reserved memory. Therefore, by assigning different data types to variables, you can store integers, decimals or characters in these variables.

Assigning Values to Variables:

Python variables do not need explicit declaration to reserve memory space. The declaration happens automatically when you assign a value to a variable. The equal sign (=) is used to assign values to variables.

The operand to the left of the = operator is the name of the variable and the operand to the right of the = operator is the value stored in the variable. For example −

```
#!/usr/bin/python


counter = 100      # An integer assignment

miles  = 1000.0    # A floating point

name   = "John"    # A string
```

```
print counter

print miles

print name
```

Here, 100, 1000.0 and "John" are the values assigned to *counter*, *miles*, and *name* variables, respectively. This produces the following result –

```
100
1000.0
John
```

Multiple Assignment:

Python allows you to assign a single value to several variables simultaneously. For example –

```
a = b = c = 1
```

Here, an integer object is created with the value 1, and all three variables are assigned to the same memory location. You can also assign multiple objects to multiple variables. For example –

```
a,b,c = 1,2,"john"
```

Here, two integer objects with values 1 and 2 are assigned to variables a and b respectively, and one string object with the value "john" is assigned to the variable c.

Standard Data Types:

The data stored in memory can be of many types. For example, a person's age is stored as a numeric value and his or her address is stored as alphanumeric characters. Python has various standard data types that are used to define the operations possible on them and the storage method for each of them.

Python has five standard data types −

- Numbers
- String
- List
- Tuple
- Dictionary

Python - Numbers

Number data types store numeric values. Number objects are created when you assign a value to them. For example –

```
var1 = 1
var2 = 10
```

You can also delete the reference to a number object by using the del statement. The syntax of the del statement is –

```
del var1[,var2[,var3[....,varN]]]]
```

You can delete a single object or multiple objects by using the del statement. For example –

```
del var
del var_a, var_b
```

Python supports four different numerical types –

- int (signed integers)
- long (long integers, they can also be represented in octal and hexadecimal)
- float (floating point real values)
- complex (complex numbers)

Examples

Here are some examples of numbers –

int	long	float	complex
10	51924361L	0.0	3.14j
100	-0x19323L	15.20	45.j
-786	0122L	-21.9	9.322e-36j
080	0xDEFABCECBDAECBFBAEl	32.3+e18	.876j
-0490	535633629843L	-90.	-.6545+0J
-0x260	-052318172735L	-32.54e100	3e+26J
0x69	-4721885298529L	70.2-E12	4.53e-7j

- Python allows you to use a lowercase l with long, but it is recommended that you use only an uppercase L to avoid confusion with the number 1. Python displays long integers with an uppercase L.

- A complex number consists of an ordered pair of real floating-point numbers denoted by x + yj, where x and y are the real numbers and j is the imaginary unit.

Python - Strings

Strings in Python are identified as a contiguous set of characters represented in the quotation marks. Python allows for either pairs of single or double quotes. Subsets of strings can be taken using the slice operator ([ ] and [:]) with indexes starting at 0 in the beginning of the string and working their way from -1 at the end.

The plus (+) sign is the string concatenation operator and the asterisk (*) is the repetition operator. For example –

```
#!/usr/bin/python


str = 'Hello World!'


print str        # Prints complete string

print str[0]     # Prints first character of the string

print str[2:5]   # Prints characters starting from 3rd to 5th

print str[2:]    # Prints string starting from 3rd character

print str * 2    # Prints string two times

print str + "TEST" # Prints concatenated string
```

This will produce the following result –

```
Hello World!
H
llo
llo World!
Hello World!Hello World!
Hello World!TEST
```

Python - Lists

Lists are the most versatile of Python's compound data types. A list contains items separated by commas and enclosed within square brackets ([]). To some extent, lists are similar to arrays in C. One difference between them is that all the items belonging to a list can be of different data type.

The values stored in a list can be accessed using the slice operator ([ ] and [:]) with indexes starting at 0 in the beginning of the list and working their way to end -1. The plus (+) sign is the list concatenation operator, and the asterisk (*) is the repetition operator. For example –

```
#!/usr/bin/python


list = [ 'abcd', 786 , 2.23, 'john', 70.2 ]
tinylist = [123, 'john']


print list        # Prints complete list
print list[0]     # Prints first element of the list
print list[1:3]   # Prints elements starting from 2nd till 3rd
print list[2:]    # Prints elements starting from 3rd element
print tinylist * 2 # Prints list two times
```

```
print list + tinylist # Prints concatenated lists
```

This produce the following result −

```
['abcd', 786, 2.23, 'john', 70.2]
abcd
[786, 2.23]
[2.23, 'john', 70.2]
[123, 'john', 123, 'john']
['abcd', 786, 2.23, 'john', 70.2, 123, 'john']
```

Python - Tuples

A tuple is another sequence data type that is similar to the list. A tuple consists of a number of values separated by commas. Unlike lists, however, tuples are enclosed within parentheses.

The main differences between lists and tuples are: Lists are enclosed in brackets ([ ]) and their elements and size can be changed, while tuples are enclosed in parentheses (( )) and cannot be updated. Tuples can be thought of as **read-only** lists. For example –

```
#!/usr/bin/python


tuple = ( 'abcd', 786 , 2.23, 'john', 70.2  )

tinytuple = (123, 'john')


print tuple        # Prints complete list

print tuple[0]      # Prints first element of the list

print tuple[1:3]      # Prints elements starting from 2nd till 3rd

print tuple[2:]        # Prints elements starting from 3rd element

print tinytuple * 2   # Prints list two times

print tuple + tinytuple # Prints concatenated lists
```

This produce the following result −

```
('abcd', 786, 2.23, 'john', 70.2)
abcd
(786, 2.23)
(2.23, 'john', 70.2)
(123, 'john', 123, 'john')
('abcd', 786, 2.23, 'john', 70.2, 123, 'john')
```

The following code is invalid with tuple, because we attempted to update a tuple, which is not allowed. Similar case is possible with lists −

```
#!/usr/bin/python


tuple = ( 'abcd', 786 , 2.23, 'john', 70.2  )

list = [ 'abcd', 786 , 2.23, 'john', 70.2  ]

tuple[2] = 1000    # Invalid syntax with tuple

list[2] = 1000     # Valid syntax with list
```

Python - Dictionary

Python's dictionaries are kind of hash table type. They work like associative arrays or hashes found in Perl and consist of key-value pairs. A dictionary key can be almost any Python type, but are usually numbers or strings. Values, on the other hand, can be any arbitrary Python object.

Dictionaries are enclosed by curly braces ({ }) and values can be assigned and accessed using square braces ([]). For example –

```python
#!/usr/bin/python

dict = {}
dict['one'] = "This is one"
dict[2]    = "This is two"


tinydict = {'name': 'john','code':6734, 'dept': 'sales'}


print dict['one']    # Prints value for 'one' key
print dict[2]        # Prints value for 2 key
print tinydict       # Prints complete dictionary
```

```
print tinydict.keys()   # Prints all the keys

print tinydict.values() # Prints all the values
```

This produce the following result −

```
This is one
This is two
{'dept': 'sales', 'code': 6734, 'name': 'john'}
['dept', 'code', 'name']
['sales', 6734, 'john']
```

Dictionaries have no concept of order among elements. It is incorrect to say that the elements are "out of order"; they are simply unordered.

Data Type Conversion:

Sometimes, you may need to perform conversions between the built-in types. To convert between types, you simply use the type name as a function.

There are several built-in functions to perform conversion from one data type to another. These functions return a new object representing the converted value.

Sr.No.	Function & Description
1	**int(x [,base])** Converts x to an integer. base specifies the base if x is a string.
2	**long(x [,base])** Converts x to a long integer. base specifies the base if x is a string.
3	**float(x)** Converts x to a floating-point number.

4	**complex(real [,imag])**
	Creates a complex number.
5	**str(x)**
	Converts object x to a string representation.
6	**repr(x)**
	Converts object x to an expression string.
7	**eval(str)**
	Evaluates a string and returns an object.
8	**tuple(s)**
	Converts s to a tuple.
9	**list(s)**
	Converts s to a list.
10	**set(s)**
	Converts s to a set.
11	**dict(d)**

	Creates a dictionary. d must be a sequence of (key,value) tuples.
12	**frozenset(s)** Converts s to a frozen set.
13	**chr(x)** Converts an integer to a character.
14	**unichr(x)** Converts an integer to a Unicode character.
15	**ord(x)** Converts a single character to its integer value.
16	**hex(x)** Converts an integer to a hexadecimal string.
17	**oct(x)** Converts an integer to an octal string.

Scope of Variables:

All variables in a program may not be accessible at all locations in that program. This depends on where you have declared a variable.

The scope of a variable determines the portion of the program where you can access a particular identifier. There are two basic scopes of variables in Python –

- Global variables
- Local variables

Global vs. Local variables

Variables that are defined inside a function body have a local scope, and those defined outside have a global scope.

This means that local variables can be accessed only inside the function in which they are declared, whereas global variables can be accessed throughout the program body by all functions. When you call a function, the variables declared inside it are brought into scope. Following is a simple example –

```
#!/usr/bin/python


total = 0; # This is global variable.
# Function definition is here
```

```
def sum( arg1, arg2 ):

    # Add both the parameters and return them."

    total = arg1 + arg2; # Here total is local variable.

    print "Inside the function local total : ", total

    return total;


# Now you can call sum function

sum( 10, 20 );

print "Outside the function global total : ", total
```

When the above code is executed, it produces the following result −

```
Inside the function local total :  30
Outside the function global total :  0
```

Python - Basic Operators

Operators are the constructs which can manipulate the value of operands.

Consider the expression 4 + 5 = 9. Here, 4 and 5 are called operands and + is called operator.

Types of Operator:

Python language supports the following types of operators.

- Arithmetic Operators
- Comparison (Relational) Operators
- Assignment Operators
- Logical Operators
- Bitwise Operators
- Membership Operators
- Identity Operators

Let us have a look on all operators one by one.

Python Arithmetic Operators:

Assume variable a holds 10 and variable b holds 20, then –

Operator	Description	Example
+ Addition	Adds values on either side of the operator.	a + b = 30
- Subtraction	Subtracts right hand operand from left hand operand.	a – b = -10
* Multiplication	Multiplies values on either side of the operator	a * b = 200
/ Division	Divides left hand operand by right hand operand	b / a = 2
% Modulus	Divides left hand operand by right hand operand and returns remainder	b % a = 0
** Exponent	Performs exponential (power) calculation on operators	a**b =10 to the

		power 20
//	Floor Division - The division of operands where the result is the quotient in which the digits after the decimal point are removed. But if one of the operands is negative, the result is floored, i.e., rounded away from zero (towards negative infinity) –	9//2 = 4 and 9.0//2.0 = 4.0, - 11//3 = - 4, 11.0//3 = -4.0

Example:

Assume variable a holds 21 and variable b holds 10, then

```
#!/usr/bin/python


a = 21

b = 10

c = 0


c = a + b

print "Line 1 - Value of c is ", c
```

```
c = a - b

print "Line 2 - Value of c is ", c


c = a * b

print "Line 3 - Value of c is ", c


c = a / b

print "Line 4 - Value of c is ", c


c = a % b

print "Line 5 - Value of c is ", c


a = 2

b = 3

c = a**b

print "Line 6 - Value of c is ", c


a = 10
```

```
b = 5

c = a//b

print "Line 7 - Value of c is ", c
```

When you execute the above program, it produces the following result −

```
Line 1 - Value of c is 31
Line 2 - Value of c is 11
Line 3 - Value of c is 210
Line 4 - Value of c is 2
Line 5 - Value of c is 1
Line 6 - Value of c is 8
Line 7 - Value of c is 2
```

Python Comparison Operators:

These operators compare the values on either sides of them and decide the relation among them. They are also called Relational operators.

Assume variable a holds 10 and variable b holds 20, then

Operator	Description	Example
==	If the values of two operands are equal, then the condition becomes true.	(a == b) is not true.
!=	If values of two operands are not equal, then condition becomes true.	(a != b) is true.
<>	If values of two operands are not equal, then condition becomes true.	(a <> b) is true. This is similar to != operator.
>	If the value of left operand is greater than the value of right operand, then condition becomes	(a > b) is not true.

	true.	
<	If the value of left operand is less than the value of right operand, then condition becomes true.	(a < b) is true.
>=	If the value of left operand is greater than or equal to the value of right operand, then condition becomes true.	(a >= b) is not true.
<=	If the value of left operand is less than or equal to the value of right operand, then condition becomes true.	(a <= b) is true.

Example:

Assume variable a holds 10 and variable b holds 20, then

```
#!/usr/bin/python


a = 21

b = 10

c = 0


if ( a == b ):

   print "Line 1 - a is equal to b"

else:

   print "Line 1 - a is not equal to b"


if ( a != b ):

   print "Line 2 - a is not equal to b"

else:

   print "Line 2 - a is equal to b"


if ( a <> b ):
```

```
   print "Line 3 - a is not equal to b"
else:
   print "Line 3 - a is equal to b"


if ( a < b ):
   print "Line 4 - a is less than b"
else:
   print "Line 4 - a is not less than b"


if ( a > b ):
   print "Line 5 - a is greater than b"
else:
   print "Line 5 - a is not greater than b"


a = 5;
b = 20;
if ( a <= b ):
   print "Line 6 - a is either less than or equal to  b"
else:
```

```
   print "Line 6 - a is neither less than nor equal to  b"



if ( b >= a ):

   print "Line 7 - b is either greater than  or equal to b"

else:

   print "Line 7 - b is neither greater than  nor equal to b"
```

When you execute the above program it produces the following result:

```
Line 1 - a is not equal to b
Line 2 - a is not equal to b
Line 3 - a is not equal to b
Line 4 - a is not less than b
Line 5 - a is greater than b
Line 6 - a is either less than or equal to b
Line 7 - b is either greater than or equal to b
```

Python Assignment Operators:

Assume variable a holds 10 and variable b holds 20, then

Operator	Description	Example
=	Assigns values from right side operands to left side operand	c = a + b assigns value of a + b into c
+= Add AND	It adds right operand to the left operand and assign the result to left operand	c += a is equivalent to c = c + a
-= Subtract AND	It subtracts right operand from the left operand and assign the result to left operand	c -= a is equivalent to c = c - a
*= Multiply AND	It multiplies right operand with the left operand and assign the result to left operand	c *= a is equivalent to c = c * a
/= Divide	It divides left operand with the	c /= a is

AND	right operand and assign the result to left operand	equivalent to c = c / ac /= a is equivalent to c = c / a
%= Modulus AND	It takes modulus using two operands and assign the result to left operand	c %= a is equivalent to c = c % a
**= Exponent AND	Performs exponential (power) calculation on operators and assign value to the left operand	c **= a is equivalent to c = c ** a
//= Floor Division	It performs floor division on operators and assign value to the left operand	c //= a is equivalent to c = c // a

Example:

Assume variable a holds 10 and variable b holds 20, then

```
#!/usr/bin/python


a = 21
b = 10
c = 0


c = a + b
print "Line 1 - Value of c is ", c


c += a
print "Line 2 - Value of c is ", c


c *= a
print "Line 3 - Value of c is ", c


c /= a
print "Line 4 - Value of c is ", c
```

```
c = 2

c %= a

print "Line 5 - Value of c is ", c


c **= a

print "Line 6 - Value of c is ", c


c //= a

print "Line 7 - Value of c is ", c
```

When you execute the above program, it produces the following result –

```
Line 1 - Value of c is 31
Line 2 - Value of c is 52
Line 3 - Value of c is 1092
Line 4 - Value of c is 52
Line 5 - Value of c is 2
Line 6 - Value of c is 2097152
Line 7 - Value of c is 99864
```

Python Bitwise Operators:

Bitwise operator works on bits and performs bit by bit operation. Assume if a = 60; and b = 13; Now in binary format they will be as follows –

a = 0011 1100

b = 0000 1101

----

a&b = 0000 1100

a|b = 0011 1101

a^b = 0011 0001

~a = 1100 0011

There are following Bitwise operators supported by Python language

Operator	Description	Example
& Binary AND	Operator copies a bit to the result if it exists in both operands	(a & b) (means 0000 1100)
| Binary OR	It copies a bit if it exists in either operand.	(a | b) = 61 (means

			0011 1101)
^ Binary XOR	It copies the bit if it is set in one operand but not both.		(a ^ b) = 49 (means 0011 0001)
~ Binary Ones Complement	It is unary and has the effect of 'flipping' bits.		(~a) = -61 (means 1100 0011 in 2's complement form due to a signed binary number.
<< Binary Left Shift	The left operands value is moved left by the number of bits specified by the right operand.		a << 2 = 240 (means 1111 0000)
>> Binary Right Shift	The left operands value is moved right by the number of bits specified by the right operand.		a >> 2 = 15 (means 0000 1111)

Example:

```
#!/usr/bin/python


a = 60        # 60 = 0011 1100

b = 13        # 13 = 0000 1101

c = 0


c = a & b;      # 12 = 0000 1100

print "Line 1 - Value of c is ", c


c = a | b;      # 61 = 0011 1101

print "Line 2 - Value of c is ", c


c = a ^ b;      # 49 = 0011 0001

print "Line 3 - Value of c is ", c


c = ~a;        # -61 = 1100 0011

print "Line 4 - Value of c is ", c
```

```
c = a << 2;      # 240 = 1111 0000

print "Line 5 - Value of c is ", c



c = a >> 2;      # 15 = 0000 1111

print "Line 6 - Value of c is ", c
```

When you execute the above program it produces the following result −

```
Line 1 - Value of c is 12
Line 2 - Value of c is 61
Line 3 - Value of c is 49
Line 4 - Value of c is -61
Line 5 - Value of c is 240
Line 6 - Value of c is 15
```

Python Logical Operators:

There are following logical operators supported by Python language. Assume variable a holds 10 and variable b holds 20 then

Operator	Description	Example
and Logical AND	If both the operands are true then condition becomes true.	(a and b) is true.
or Logical OR	If any of the two operands are non-zero then condition becomes true.	(a or b) is true.
not Logical NOT	Used to reverse the logical state of its operand.	Not(a and b) is false.

Python Membership Operators:

Python's membership operators test for membership in a sequence, such as strings, lists, or tuples. There are two membership operators as explained below

Operator	Description	Example
in	Evaluates to true if it finds a variable in the specified sequence and false otherwise.	x in y, here in results in a 1 if x is a member of sequence y.
not in	Evaluates to true if it does not finds a variable in the specified sequence and false otherwise.	x not in y, here not in results in a 1 if x is not a member of sequence y.

Example:

```
#!/usr/bin/python


a = 10
b = 20
list = [1, 2, 3, 4, 5 ];


if ( a in list ):
   print "Line 1 - a is available in the given list"
else:
   print "Line 1 - a is not available in the given list"


if ( b not in list ):
   print "Line 2 - b is not available in the given list"
else:
   print "Line 2 - b is available in the given list"


a = 2
if ( a in list ):
```

```
    print "Line 3 - a is available in the given list"
else:
    print "Line 3 - a is not available in the given list"
```

When you execute the above program it produces the following result –

```
Line 1 - a is not available in the given list
Line 2 - b is not available in the given list
Line 3 - a is available in the given list
```

Python Identity Operators:

Identity operators compare the memory locations of two objects. There are two Identity operators explained below

Operator	Description	Example
is	Evaluates to true if the variables on either side of the operator point to the same object and false otherwise.	x is y, here **is** results in 1 if id(x) equals id(y).
is not	Evaluates to false if the variables on either side of the operator point to the same object and true otherwise.	x is not y, here **is not**results in 1 if id(x) is not equal to id(y).

Example:

```
#!/usr/bin/python


a = 20
b = 20
```

```
if ( a is b ):

   print "Line 1 - a and b have same identity"

else:

   print "Line 1 - a and b do not have same identity"


if ( id(a) == id(b) ):

   print "Line 2 - a and b have same identity"

else:

   print "Line 2 - a and b do not have same identity"


b = 30

if ( a is b ):

   print "Line 3 - a and b have same identity"

else:

   print "Line 3 - a and b do not have same identity"


if ( a is not b ):

   print "Line 4 - a and b do not have same identity"

else:
```

```
print "Line 4 - a and b have same identity"
```

When you execute the above program it produces the following result −

```
Line 1 - a and b have same identity
Line 2 - a and b have same identity
Line 3 - a and b do not have same identity
Line 4 - a and b do not have same identity
```

Python Operators Precedence:

The following table lists all operators from highest precedence to lowest.

Sr.No.	Operator & Description
1	** Exponentiation (raise to the power)
2	~ + - Complement, unary plus and minus (method names for the last two are +@ and -@)
3	* / % // Multiply, divide, modulo and floor division
4	+ - Addition and subtraction
5	>> << Right and left bitwise shift
6	&

	Bitwise 'AND'	
7	^ | Bitwise exclusive `OR' and regular `OR'	
8	<= < > >= Comparison operators	
9	<> == != Equality operators	
10	= %= /= //= -= += *= **= Assignment operators	
11	**is is not** Identity operators	
12	**in not in** Membership operators	
13	**not or and** Logical operators	

Operator precedence affects how an expression is evaluated.

For example, x = 7 + 3 * 2; here, x is assigned 13, not 20 because operator * has higher precedence than +, so it first multiplies 3*2 and then adds into 7.

Here, operators with the highest precedence appear at the top of the table, those with the lowest appear at the bottom.

Example:

```
#!/usr/bin/python


a = 20

b = 10

c = 15

d = 5

e = 0


e = (a + b) * c / d     #( 30 * 15 ) / 5

print "Value of (a + b) * c / d is ", e
```

```
e = ((a + b) * c) / d    # (30 * 15 ) / 5

print "Value of ((a + b) * c) / d is ",  e


e = (a + b) * (c / d);   # (30) * (15/5)

print "Value of (a + b) * (c / d) is ",  e


e = a + (b * c) / d;     # 20 + (150/5)

print "Value of a + (b * c) / d is ",  e
```

When you execute the above program, it produces the following result –

```
Value of (a + b) * c / d is 90

Value of ((a + b) * c) / d is 90

Value of (a + b) * (c / d) is 90

Value of a + (b * c) / d is 50
```

Python - Decision Making

Decision making is anticipation of conditions occurring while execution of the program and specifying actions taken according to the conditions.

Decision structures evaluate multiple expressions which produce TRUE or FALSE as outcome. You need to determine which action to take and which statements to execute if outcome is TRUE or FALSE otherwise.

Following is the general form of a typical decision making structure found in most of the programming languages –

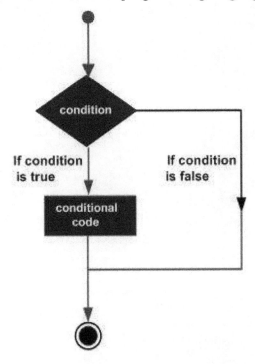

Python programming language assumes any **non-zero** and **non-null** values as TRUE, and if it is either **zero** or **null**, then it is assumed as FALSE value.

Python programming language provides following types of decision making statements. Click the following links to check their detail.

Sr.No.	Statement & Description
1	**if statements** An **if statement** consists of a boolean expression followed by one or more statements.
2	**if...else statements** An **if statement** can be followed by an optional **else statement**, which executes when the boolean expression is FALSE.
3	**nested if statements** You can use one **if** or **else if** statement inside another **if** or **else if** statement(s).

Let us go through each decision making briefly −

If statements:

It is similar to that of other languages. The **if** statement contains a logical expression using which data is compared and a decision is made based on the result of the comparison.

Syntax:

```
if expression:
   statement(s)
```

If the boolean expression evaluates to TRUE, then the block of statement(s) inside the if statement is executed. If boolean expression evaluates to FALSE, then the first set of code after the end of the if statement(s) is executed.

Flow Diagram:

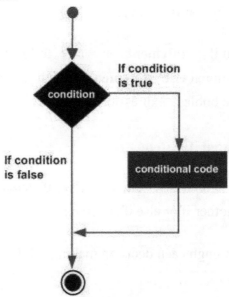

Example:

```
#!/usr/bin/python


var1 = 100
if var1:
   print "1 - Got a true expression value"
   print var1

var2 = 0
if var2:
   print "2 - Got a true expression value"
   print var2
print "Good bye!"
```

When the above code is executed, it produces the following result –

```
1 - Got a true expression value
100
Good bye!
```

if...else statements:

An **else** statement can be combined with an **if** statement. An **else** statement contains the block of code that executes if the conditional expression in the if statement resolves to 0 or a FALSE value.

The *else* statement is an optional statement and there could be at most only one **else** statement following **if**.

Syntax:

The syntax of the *if...else* statement is –

```
if expression:
   statement(s)
else:
   statement(s)
```

Flow Diagram:

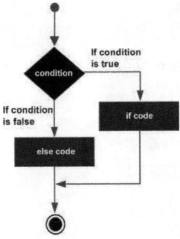

Example

```
#!/usr/bin/python


var1 = 100
if var1:
   print "1 - Got a true expression value"
   print var1
else:
   print "1 - Got a false expression value"
   print var1


var2 = 0
if var2:
   print "2 - Got a true expression value"
   print var2
else:
   print "2 - Got a false expression value"
   print var2
```

```
print "Good bye!"
```

When the above code is executed, it produces the following result −

```
1 - Got a true expression value
100
2 - Got a false expression value
0
Good bye!
```

The *elif* Statement:

The **elif** statement allows you to check multiple expressions for TRUE and execute a block of code as soon as one of the conditions evaluates to TRUE.

Similar to the **else**, the **elif** statement is optional. However, unlike **else**, for which there can be at most one statement, there can be an arbitrary number of **elif** statements following an **if**.

syntax

```
if expression1:
   statement(s)
elif expression2:
   statement(s)
elif expression3:
   statement(s)
else:
   statement(s)
```

Core Python does not provide switch or case statements as in other languages, but we can use if..elif...statements to simulate switch case as follows –

Example

```
#!/usr/bin/python


var = 100
if var == 200:
    print "1 - Got a true expression value"
    print var
elif var == 150:
    print "2 - Got a true expression value"
    print var
elif var == 100:
    print "3 - Got a true expression value"
    print var
else:
    print "4 - Got a false expression value"
    print var
```

```
print "Good bye!"
```

When the above code is executed, it produces the following result –

```
3 - Got a true expression value
100
Good bye!
```

nested if statements:

There may be a situation when you want to check for another condition after a condition resolves to true. In such a situation, you can use the nested **if** construct.

In a nested **if** construct, you can have an **if...elif...else**construct inside another **if...elif...else** construct.

Syntax:

The syntax of the nested *if...elif...else* construct may be −

```
if expression1:
   statement(s)
   if expression2:
     statement(s)
   elif expression3:
     statement(s)
   elif expression4:
     statement(s)
   else:
     statement(s)
else:
   statement(s)
```

Example

```
#!/usr/bin/python


var = 100
```

```
if var < 200:

   print "Expression value is less than 200"

   if var == 150:

      print "Which is 150"

   elif var == 100:

      print "Which is 100"

   elif var == 50:

      print "Which is 50"

   elif var < 50:

      print "Expression value is less than 50"

else:

   print "Could not find true expression"


print "Good bye!"
```

When the above code is executed, it produces following result −

```
Expression value is less than 200
Which is 100
Good bye!
```

Single Statement Suites:

If the suite of an **if** clause consists only of a single line, it may go on the same line as the header statement.

Here is an example of a **one-line if** clause −

```
#!/usr/bin/python


var = 100
if ( var == 100 ) : print "Value of expression is 100"
print "Good bye!"
```

When the above code is executed, it produces the following result −

```
Value of expression is 100
Good bye!
```

Python – Loops

In general, statements are executed sequentially: The first statement in a function is executed first, followed by the second, and so on. There may be a situation when you need to execute a block of code several number of times.

Programming languages provide various control structures that allow for more complicated execution paths.

A loop statement allows us to execute a statement or group of statements multiple times. The following diagram illustrates a loop statement:

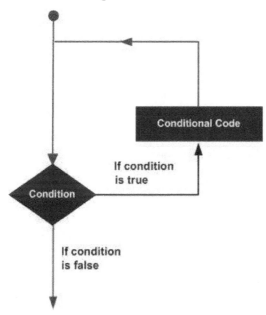

Python programming language provides following types of loops to handle looping requirements.

Sr.No.	Loop Type & Description
1	**while loop** Repeats a statement or group of statements while a given condition is TRUE. It tests the condition before executing the loop body.
2	**for loop** Executes a sequence of statements multiple times and abbreviates the code that manages the loop variable.
3	**nested loops** You can use one or more loop inside any another while, for or do..while loop.

While loop:

A **while** loop statement in Python programming language repeatedly executes a target statement as long as a given condition is true.

Syntax:

The syntax of a **while** loop in Python programming language is −

```
while expression:
   statement(s)
```

Here, **statement(s)** may be a single statement or a block of statements. The **condition** may be any expression, and true is any non-zero value. The loop iterates while the condition is true.

When the condition becomes false, program control passes to the line immediately following the loop.

In Python, all the statements indented by the same number of character spaces after a programming construct are considered to be part of a single block of code. Python uses indentation as its method of grouping statements.

Flow Diagram:

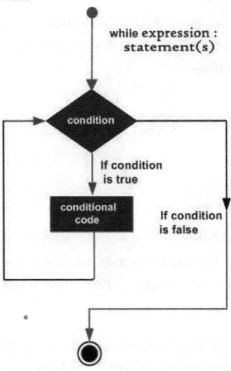

Here, key point of the while loop is that the loop might not ever run. When the condition is tested and the result is false, the loop body will be skipped and the first statement after the while loop will be executed.

Example:

```
#!/usr/bin/python


count = 0
while (count < 9):
    print 'The count is:', count
    count = count + 1


print "Good bye!"
```

When the above code is executed, it produces the following result –

```
The count is: 0
The count is: 1
The count is: 2
The count is: 3
The count is: 4
The count is: 5
The count is: 6
The count is: 7
The count is: 8
Good bye!
```

The block here, consisting of the print and increment statements, is executed repeatedly until count is no longer less than 9. With each iteration, the current value of the index count is displayed and then increased by 1.

For loop:

It has the ability to iterate over the items of any sequence, such as a list or a string.

Syntax:

```
for iterating_var in sequence:
   statements(s)
```

If a sequence contains an expression list, it is evaluated first. Then, the first item in the sequence is assigned to the iterating variable *iterating_var*. Next, the statements block is executed. Each item in the list is assigned to *iterating_var*, and the statement(s) block is executed until the entire sequence is exhausted.

Flow Diagram:

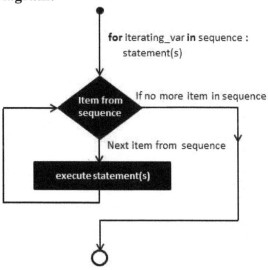

Example

```
#!/usr/bin/python


for letter in 'Python':    # First Example

  print 'Current Letter :', letter


fruits = ['banana', 'apple',  'mango']

for fruit in fruits:        # Second Example

  print 'Current fruit :', fruit
```

```
print "Good bye!"
```

When the above code is executed, it produces the following result −

```
Current Letter : P
Current Letter : y
Current Letter : t
Current Letter : h
Current Letter : o
Current Letter : n
Current fruit : banana
Current fruit : apple
Current fruit : mango
Good bye!
```

nested loops:

Python programming language allows to use one loop inside another loop. Following section shows few examples to illustrate the concept.

Syntax

```
for iterating_var in sequence:
  for iterating_var in sequence:
    statements(s)
  statements(s)
```

The syntax for a **nested while loop** statement in Python programming language is as follows –

```
while expression:
  while expression:
    statement(s)
  statement(s)
```

A final note on loop nesting is that you can put any type of loop inside of any other type of loop. For example a for loop can be inside a while loop or vice versa.

Example:

The following program uses a nested for loop to find the prime numbers from 2 to 100 –

```
#!/usr/bin/python


i = 2

while(i < 100):

  j = 2

  while(j <= (i/j)):

    if not(i%j): break

    j = j + 1

  if (j > i/j) : print i, " is prime"

  i = i + 1
```

```
print "Good bye!"
```

When the above code is executed, it produces following result –

```
2 is prime
3 is prime
5 is prime
7 is prime
11 is prime
13 is prime
17 is prime
19 is prime
23 is prime
29 is prime
31 is prime
37 is prime
41 is prime
43 is prime
47 is prime
53 is prime
59 is prime
61 is prime
67 is prime
71 is prime
73 is prime
79 is prime
83 is prime
89 is prime
97 is prime
Good bye!
```

Loop Control Statements:

Loop control statements change execution from its normal sequence. When execution leaves a scope, all automatic objects that were created in that scope are destroyed.

Python supports the following control statements. Click the following links to check their detail.

Let us go through the loop control statements briefly

Sr.No.	Control Statement & Description
1	**break statement** Terminates the loop statement and transfers execution to the statement immediately following the loop.
2	**continue statement** Causes the loop to skip the remainder of its body and immediately retest its condition prior to reiterating.
3	**pass statement** The pass statement in Python is used when a statement is required syntactically but you do not

want any command or code to execute.

Break statement:

It terminates the current loop and resumes execution at the next statement, just like the traditional break statement in C.

The most common use for break is when some external condition is triggered requiring a hasty exit from a loop. The **break** statement can be used in both *while* and *for* loops.

If you are using nested loops, the break statement stops the execution of the innermost loop and start executing the next line of code after the block.

Syntax:

The syntax for a **break** statement in Python is as follows −

```
break
```

Flow Diagram:

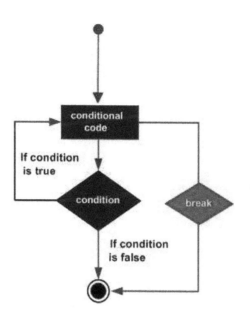

Example:

```
#!/usr/bin/python


for letter in 'Python':    # First Example
  if letter == 'h':
    break
  print 'Current Letter :', letter
```

```
var = 10              # Second Example

while var > 0:

    print 'Current variable value :', var

    var = var -1

    if var == 5:

        break


print "Good bye!"
```

When the above code is executed, it produces the following result −

```
Current Letter : P
Current Letter : y
Current Letter : t
Current variable value : 10
Current variable value : 9
Current variable value : 8
Current variable value : 7
Current variable value : 6
Good bye!
```

Continue statement:

It returns the control to the beginning of the while loop.. The **continue** statement rejects all the remaining statements in the current iteration of the loop and moves the control back to the top of the loop.

The **continue** statement can be used in both *while* and *for* loops.

Syntax

```
continue
```

Flow Diagram:

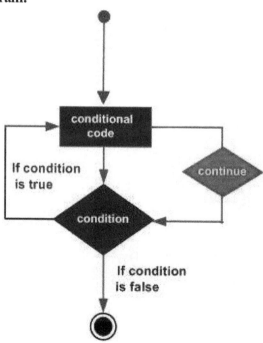

Example:

```
#!/usr/bin/python


for letter in 'Python':    # First Example
   if letter == 'h':
      continue
   print 'Current Letter :', letter


var = 10               # Second Example
while var > 0:
   var = var -1
   if var == 5:
      continue
   print 'Current variable value :', var
print "Good bye!"
```

When the above code is executed, it produces the following result −

```
Current Letter : P
Current Letter : y
Current Letter : t
```

```
Current Letter : o
Current Letter : n
Current variable value : 9
Current variable value : 8
Current variable value : 7
Current variable value : 6
Current variable value : 4
Current variable value : 3
Current variable value : 2
Current variable value : 1
Current variable value : 0
Good bye!
```

Pass statement:

It is used when a statement is required syntactically but you do not want any command or code to execute.

The **pass** statement is a *null* operation; nothing happens when it executes. The **pass** is also useful in places where your code will eventually go, but has not been written yet (e.g., in stubs for example) –

Syntax

```
pass
```

Example

```
#!/usr/bin/python

for letter in 'Python':
   if letter == 'h':
      pass
      print 'This is pass block'
   print 'Current Letter :', letter

print "Good bye!"
```

When the above code is executed, it produces following result −

```
Current Letter : P
Current Letter : y
Current Letter : t
This is pass block
Current Letter : h
Current Letter : o
Current Letter : n
Good bye!
```

Python – Numbers

Number data types store numeric values. They are immutable data types, means that changing the value of a number data type results in a newly allocated object.

Number objects are created when you assign a value to them. For example −

```
var1 = 1
var2 = 10
```

You can also delete the reference to a number object by using the **del** statement. The syntax of the del statement is −

```
del var1[,var2[,var3[....,varN]]]]
```

You can delete a single object or multiple objects by using the **del** statement. For example −

```
del var
del var_a, var_b
```

Python supports four different numerical types −

- **int (signed integers)** − They are often called just integers or ints, are positive or negative whole numbers with no decimal point.

- **long (long integers)** − Also called longs, they are integers of unlimited size, written like integers and followed by an uppercase or lowercase L.

- **float (floating point real values)** – Also called floats, they represent real numbers and are written with a decimal point dividing the integer and fractional parts. Floats may also be in scientific notation, with E or e indicating the power of 10 ($2.5e2 = 2.5 \times 10^2 = 250$).

- **complex (complex numbers)** – are of the form a + bJ, where a and b are floats and J (or j) represents the square root of -1 (which is an imaginary number). The real part of the number is a, and the imaginary part is b. Complex numbers are not used much in Python programming.

Examples

Here are some examples of numbers

int	long	float	complex
10	51924361L	0.0	3.14j
100	-0x19323L	15.20	45.j
-786	0122L	-21.9	9.322e-36j

080	0xDEFABCECBDAECBFBAEL	32.3+e18	.876j
-0490	535633629843L	-90.	-.6545+0J
-0x260	-052318172735L	-32.54e100	3e+26J
0x69	-4721885298529L	70.2-E12	4.53e-7j

- Python allows you to use a lowercase L with long, but it is recommended that you use only an uppercase L to avoid confusion with the number 1. Python displays long integers with an uppercase L.

- A complex number consists of an ordered pair of real floating point numbers denoted by a + bj, where a is the real part and b is the imaginary part of the complex number.

Number Type Conversion:

Python converts numbers internally in an expression containing mixed types to a common type for evaluation. But sometimes, you need to coerce a number explicitly from one type to another to satisfy the requirements of an operator or function parameter.

- Type **int(x)** to convert x to a plain integer.

- Type **long(x)** to convert x to a long integer.

- Type **float(x)** to convert x to a floating-point number.

- Type **complex(x)** to convert x to a complex number with real part x and imaginary part zero.

- Type **complex(x, y)** to convert x and y to a complex number with real part x and imaginary part y. x and y are numeric expressions

Mathematical Functions

Python includes following functions that perform mathematical calculations.

Sr.No.	Function & Returns (description)
1	**abs(x)** The absolute value of x: the (positive) distance between x and zero.
2	**ceil(x)** The ceiling of x: the smallest integer not less than x
3	**cmp(x, y)** -1 if x < y, 0 if x == y, or 1 if x > y
4	**exp(x)** The exponential of x: e^x
5	**fabs(x)** The absolute value of x.

6	**floor(x)**
	The floor of x: the largest integer not greater than x
7	**log(x)**
	The natural logarithm of x, for x> 0
8	**log10(x)**
	The base-10 logarithm of x for x> 0.
9	**max(x1, x2,...)**
	The largest of its arguments: the value closest to positive infinity
10	**min(x1, x2,...)**
	The smallest of its arguments: the value closest to negative infinity
11	**modf(x)**
	The fractional and integer parts of x in a two-item tuple. Both parts have the same sign as x. The integer part is returned as a float.

12	**pow(x, y)** The value of x**y.
13	**round(x [,n])** x rounded to n digits from the decimal point. Python rounds away from zero as a tie-breaker: round(0.5) is 1.0 and round(-0.5) is -1.0.
14	**sqrt(x)** The square root of x for x > 0

Random Number Functions:

Random numbers are used for games, simulations, testing, security, and privacy applications. Python includes following functions that are commonly used.

Sr.No.	Function & Description
1	**choice(seq)** A random item from a list, tuple, or string.

2	**randrange ([start,] stop [,step])**
	A randomly selected element from range(start, stop, step)
3	**random()**
	A random float r, such that 0 is less than or equal to r and r is less than 1
4	**seed([x])**
	Sets the integer starting value used in generating random numbers. Call this function before calling any other random module function. Returns None.
5	**shuffle(lst)**
	Randomizes the items of a list in place. Returns None.
6	**uniform(x, y)**
	A random float r, such that x is less than or equal to r and r is less than y

Trigonometric Functions:

Python includes following functions that perform trigonometric calculations.

Sr.No.	Function & Description
1	**acos(x)**
	Return the arc cosine of x, in radians.
2	**asin(x)**
	Return the arc sine of x, in radians.
3	**atan(x)**
	Return the arc tangent of x, in radians.
4	**atan2(y, x)**
	Return atan(y / x), in radians.
5	**cos(x)**
	Return the cosine of x radians.
6	**hypot(x, y)**

	Return the Euclidean norm, sqrt(x*x + y*y).
7	**sin(x)** Return the sine of x radians.
8	**tan(x)** Return the tangent of x radians.
9	**degrees(x)** Converts angle x from radians to degrees.
10	**radians(x)** Converts angle x from degrees to radians.

Mathematical Constants:

The module also defines two mathematical constants –

Sr.No.	Constants & Description
1	**pi** The mathematical constant pi.
2	**e** The mathematical constant e.

Python – Strings

Strings are amongst the most popular types in Python. We can create them simply by enclosing characters in quotes. Python treats single quotes the same as double quotes. Creating strings is as simple as assigning a value to a variable. For example −

```
var1 = 'Hello World!'

var2 = "Python Programming"
```

Accessing Values in Strings:

Python does not support a character type; these are treated as strings of length one, thus also considered a substring.

To access substrings, use the square brackets for slicing along with the index or indices to obtain your substring. For example −

```
#!/usr/bin/python


var1 = 'Hello World!'

var2 = "Python Programming"


print "var1[0]: ", var1[0]

print "var2[1:5]: ", var2[1:5]
```

When the above code is executed, it produces the following result –

```
var1[0]:  H
var2[1:5]:  ytho
```

Updating Strings:

You can "update" an existing string by (re)assigning a variable to another string. The new value can be related to its previous value or to a completely different string altogether. For example –

```
#!/usr/bin/python


var1 = 'Hello World!'

print "Updated String :- ", var1[:6] + 'Python'
```

When the above code is executed, it produces the following result –

```
Updated String :-  Hello Python
```

Escape Characters:

Following table is a list of escape or non-printable characters that can be represented with backslash notation.

An escape character gets interpreted; in a single quoted as well as double quoted strings.

Backslash notation	Hexadecimal character	Description
\a	0x07	Bell or alert
\b	0x08	Backspace
\cx		Control-x
\C-x		Control-x
\e	0x1b	Escape
\f	0x0c	Formfeed
\M-\C-x		Meta-Control-x
\n	0x0a	Newline

\nnn		Octal notation, where n is in the range 0.7
\r	0x0d	Carriage return
\s	0x20	Space
\t	0x09	Tab
\v	0x0b	Vertical tab
\x		Character x
\xnn		Hexadecimal notation, where n is in the range 0.9, a.f, or A.F

String Special Operators:

Assume string variable **a** holds 'Hello' and variable **b** holds 'Python', then –

Operator	Description	Example
+	Concatenation - Adds values on either side of the operator	a + b will give HelloPython
*	Repetition - Creates new strings, concatenating multiple copies of the same string	a*2 will give - HelloHello
[]	Slice - Gives the character from the given index	a[1] will give e
[:]	Range Slice - Gives the characters from the given range	a[1:4] will give ell
in	Membership - Returns true if a character exists in the given string	H in a will give 1

not in	Membership - Returns true if a character does not exist in the given string	M not in a will give 1
r/R	Raw String - Suppresses actual meaning of Escape characters. The syntax for raw strings is exactly the same as for normal strings with the exception of the raw string operator, the letter "r," which precedes the quotation marks. The "r" can be lowercase (r) or uppercase (R) and must be placed immediately preceding the first quote mark.	print r'\n' prints \n and print R'\n'prints \n
%	Format - Performs String formatting	See at next section

String Formatting Operator

One of Python's coolest features is the string format operator %. This operator is unique to strings and makes up for the pack of having functions from C's printf() family. Following is a simple example –

```
#!/usr/bin/python


print "My name is %s and weight is %d kg!" % ('Zara', 21)
```

When the above code is executed, it produces the following result –

```
My name is Zara and weight is 21 kg!
```

Here is the list of complete set of symbols which can be used along with % –

Format Symbol	Conversion
%c	character
%s	string conversion via str() prior to formatting

%i	signed decimal integer
%d	signed decimal integer
%u	unsigned decimal integer
%o	octal integer
%x	hexadecimal integer (lowercase letters)
%X	hexadecimal integer (UPPERcase letters)
%e	exponential notation (with lowercase 'e')
%E	exponential notation (with UPPERcase 'E')
%f	floating point real number
%g	the shorter of %f and %e

%G	the shorter of %f and %E

Other supported symbols and functionality are listed in the following table –

Symbol	Functionality
*	argument specifies width or precision
-	left justification
+	display the sign
<sp>	leave a blank space before a positive number
#	add the octal leading zero ('0') or hexadecimal leading '0x' or '0X', depending on whether 'x' or 'X' were used.
0	pad from left with zeros (instead of spaces)

%	'%%' leaves you with a single literal '%'
(var)	mapping variable (dictionary arguments)
m.n.	m is the minimum total width and n is the number of digits to display after the decimal point (if appl.)

Triple Quotes:

Python's triple quotes comes to the rescue by allowing strings to span multiple lines, including verbatim NEWLINEs, TABs, and any other special characters.

The syntax for triple quotes consists of three consecutive **single or double** quotes.

```
#!/usr/bin/python


para_str = """this is a long string that is made up of

several lines and non-printable characters such as

TAB ( \t ) and they will show up that way when displayed.

NEWLINEs within the string, whether explicitly given like

this within the brackets [ \n ], or just a NEWLINE within
```

```
the variable assignment will also show up.

"""

print para_str
```

When the above code is executed, it produces the following result. Note how every single special character has been converted to its printed form, right down to the last NEWLINE at the end of the string between the "up." and closing triple quotes. Also note that NEWLINEs occur either with an explicit carriage return at the end of a line or its escape code (\n) −

```
this is a long string that is made up of
several lines and non-printable characters such as
TAB (   ) and they will show up that way when displayed.
NEWLINEs within the string, whether explicitly given like
this within the brackets [
], or just a NEWLINE within
the variable assignment will also show up.
```

Raw strings do not treat the backslash as a special character at all. Every character you put into a raw string stays the way you wrote it −

```
#!/usr/bin/python


print 'C:\\nowhere'
```

When the above code is executed, it produces the following result −

```
C:\nowhere
```

Now let's make use of raw string. We would put expression in **r'expression'** as follows −

```
#!/usr/bin/python


print r'C;\\nowhere'
```

When the above code is executed, it produces the following result −

```
C:\\nowhere
```

Unicode String:

Normal strings in Python are stored internally as 8-bit ASCII, while Unicode strings are stored as 16-bit Unicode. This allows for a more varied set of characters, including special characters from most languages in the world. I'll restrict my treatment of Unicode strings to the following −

```
#!/usr/bin/python


print u'Hello, world!'
```

When the above code is executed, it produces the following result −

Hello, world!

As you can see, Unicode strings use the prefix u, just as raw strings use the prefix r.

Built-in String Methods:

Python includes the following built-in methods to manipulate strings −

Sr.No.	Methods with Description
1	**capitalize()** Capitalizes first letter of string
2	**center(width, fillchar)** Returns a space-padded string with the original string centered to a total of width columns.

3	count(str, beg= 0,end=len(string))
	Counts how many times str occurs in string or in a substring of string if starting index beg and ending index end are given.
4	decode(encoding='UTF-8',errors='strict')
	Decodes the string using the codec registered for encoding. encoding defaults to the default string encoding.
5	encode(encoding='UTF-8',errors='strict')
	Returns encoded string version of string; on error, default is to raise a ValueError unless errors is given with 'ignore' or 'replace'.
6	endswith(suffix, beg=0, end=len(string))
	Determines if string or a substring of string (if starting index beg and ending index end are given) ends with suffix; returns true if so and false otherwise.
7	expandtabs(tabsize=8)
	Expands tabs in string to multiple spaces;

	defaults to 8 spaces per tab if tabsize not provided.
8	**find(str, beg=0 end=len(string))**
	Determine if str occurs in string or in a substring of string if starting index beg and ending index end are given returns index if found and -1 otherwise.
9	**index(str, beg=0, end=len(string))**
	Same as find(), but raises an exception if str not found.
10	**isalnum()**
	Returns true if string has at least 1 character and all characters are alphanumeric and false otherwise.
11	**isalpha()**
	Returns true if string has at least 1 character and all characters are alphabetic and false otherwise.
12	**isdigit()**

	Returns true if string contains only digits and false otherwise.
13	**islower()**
	Returns true if string has at least 1 cased character and all cased characters are in lowercase and false otherwise.
14	**isnumeric()**
	Returns true if a unicode string contains only numeric characters and false otherwise.
15	**isspace()**
	Returns true if string contains only whitespace characters and false otherwise.
16	**istitle()**
	Returns true if string is properly "titlecased" and false otherwise.
17	**isupper()**
	Returns true if string has at least one cased character and all cased characters are in

	uppercase and false otherwise.
18	**join(seq)** Merges (concatenates) the string representations of elements in sequence seq into a string, with separator string.
19	**len(string)** Returns the length of the string
20	**ljust(width[, fillchar])** Returns a space-padded string with the original string left-justified to a total of width columns.
21	**lower()** Converts all uppercase letters in string to lowercase.
22	**lstrip()** Removes all leading whitespace in string.
23	**maketrans()** Returns a translation table to be used in translate

	function.
24	**max(str)**
	Returns the max alphabetical character from the string str.
25	**min(str)**
	Returns the min alphabetical character from the string str.
26	**replace(old, new [, max])**
	Replaces all occurrences of old in string with new or at most max occurrences if max given.
27	**rfind(str, beg=0,end=len(string))**
	Same as find(), but search backwards in string.
28	**rindex(str, beg=0, end=len(string))**
	Same as index(), but search backwards in string.
29	**rjust(width,[, fillchar])**
	Returns a space-padded string with the original

	string right-justified to a total of width columns.
30	**rstrip()** Removes all trailing whitespace of string.
31	**split(str="", num=string.count(str))** Splits string according to delimiter str (space if not provided) and returns list of substrings; split into at most num substrings if given.
32	**splitlines(num=string.count('\n'))** Splits string at all (or num) NEWLINEs and returns a list of each line with NEWLINEs removed.
33	**startswith(str, beg=0,end=len(string))** Determines if string or a substring of string (if starting index beg and ending index end are given) starts with substring str; returns true if so and false otherwise.
34	**strip([chars])** Performs both lstrip() and rstrip() on string.

35	swapcase()
	Inverts case for all letters in string.
36	title()
	Returns "titlecased" version of string, that is, all words begin with uppercase and the rest are lowercase.
37	translate(table, deletechars="")
	Translates string according to translation table str(256 chars), removing those in the del string.
38	upper()
	Converts lowercase letters in string to uppercase.
39	zfill (width)
	Returns original string leftpadded with zeros to a total of width characters; intended for numbers, zfill() retains any sign given (less one zero).
40	isdecimal() Returns true if a unicode string contains only decimal characters and false otherwise.

Python – Lists

The most basic data structure in Python is the **sequence**. Each element of a sequence is assigned a number - its position or index. The first index is zero, the second index is one, and so forth.

Python has six built-in types of sequences, but the most common ones are lists and tuples, which we would see in this tutorial.

There are certain things you can do with all sequence types. These operations include indexing, slicing, adding, multiplying, and checking for membership. In addition, Python has built-in functions for finding the length of a sequence and for finding its largest and smallest elements.

Python Lists

The list is a most versatile datatype available in Python which can be written as a list of comma-separated values (items) between square brackets. Important thing about a list is that items in a list need not be of the same type.

Creating a list is as simple as putting different comma-separated values between square brackets. For example –

```
list1 = ['physics', 'chemistry', 1997, 2000];
list2 = [1, 2, 3, 4, 5 ];
list3 = ["a", "b", "c", "d"]
```

Similar to string indices, list indices start at 0, and lists can be sliced, concatenated and so on.

Accessing Values in Lists:

To access values in lists, use the square brackets for slicing along with the index or indices to obtain value available at that index. For example –

```
#!/usr/bin/python


list1 = ['physics', 'chemistry', 1997, 2000];

list2 = [1, 2, 3, 4, 5, 6, 7 ];

print "list1[0]: ", list1[0]

print "list2[1:5]: ", list2[1:5]
```

When the above code is executed, it produces the following result –

```
list1[0]:  physics
list2[1:5]:  [2, 3, 4, 5]
```

Updating Lists

You can update single or multiple elements of lists by giving the slice on the left-hand side of the assignment operator, and you can add to elements in a list with the append() method. For example –

```
#!/usr/bin/python

list = ['physics', 'chemistry', 1997, 2000];
print "Value available at index 2 : "
print list[2]
list[2] = 2001;
print "New value available at index 2 : "
print list[2]
```

Note − append() method is discussed in subsequent section.

When the above code is executed, it produces the following result −

```
Value available at index 2 :
1997
New value available at index 2 :
2001
```

Delete List Elements

To remove a list element, you can use either the del statement if you know exactly which element(s) you are deleting or the remove() method if you do not know. For example −

```
#!/usr/bin/python


list1 = ['physics', 'chemistry', 1997, 2000];

print list1

del list1[2];

print "After deleting value at index 2 : "

print list1
```

When the above code is executed, it produces following result –

```
['physics', 'chemistry', 1997, 2000]
After deleting value at index 2 :
['physics', 'chemistry', 2000]
```

Note – remove() method is discussed in subsequent section.

Basic List Operations

Lists respond to the + and * operators much like strings; they mean concatenation and repetition here too, except that the result is a new list, not a string.

In fact, lists respond to all of the general sequence operations we used on strings in the prior chapter.

Python Expression	Results	Description
len([1, 2, 3])	3	Length
[1, 2, 3] + [4, 5, 6]	[1, 2, 3, 4, 5, 6]	Concatenation
['Hi!'] * 4	['Hi!', 'Hi!', 'Hi!', 'Hi!']	Repetition
3 in [1, 2, 3]	True	Membership
for x in [1, 2, 3]: print x,	1 2 3	Iteration

Indexing, Slicing, and Matrixes:

Because lists are sequences, indexing and slicing work the same way for lists as they do for strings.

Assuming following input −

L = ['spam', 'Spam', 'SPAM!']		
Python Expression	**Results**	**Description**
L[2]	SPAM!	Offsets start at zero
L[-2]	Spam	Negative: count from the right
L[1:]	['Spam', 'SPAM!']	Slicing fetches sections

Built-in List Functions & Methods:

Python includes the following list functions –

Sr.No.	Function with Description
1	**cmp(list1, list2)** Compares elements of both lists.
2	**len(list)**

	Gives the total length of the list.
3	**max(list)** Returns item from the list with max value.
4	**min(list)** Returns item from the list with min value.
5	**list(seq)** Converts a tuple into list.

Python includes following list methods

Sr.No.	Methods with Description
1	**list.append(obj)** Appends object obj to list
2	**list.count(obj)** Returns count of how many times obj occurs in list

3	**list.extend(seq)**
	Appends the contents of seq to list
4	**list.index(obj)**
	Returns the lowest index in list that obj appears
5	**list.insert(index, obj)**
	Inserts object obj into list at offset index
6	**list.pop(obj=list[-1])**
	Removes and returns last object or obj from list
7	**list.remove(obj)**
	Removes object obj from list
8	**list.reverse()**
	Reverses objects of list in place
9	**list.sort([func])**
	Sorts objects of list, use compare func if given

Python – Tuples

A tuple is a sequence of immutable Python objects. Tuples are sequences, just like lists. The differences between tuples and lists are, the tuples cannot be changed unlike lists and tuples use parentheses, whereas lists use square brackets.

Creating a tuple is as simple as putting different comma-separated values. Optionally you can put these comma-separated values between parentheses also. For example –

```
tup1 = ('physics', 'chemistry', 1997, 2000);
tup2 = (1, 2, 3, 4, 5 );
tup3 = "a", "b", "c", "d";
```

The empty tuple is written as two parentheses containing nothing –

```
tup1 = ();
```

To write a tuple containing a single value you have to include a comma, even though there is only one value –

```
tup1 = (50,);
```

Like string indices, tuple indices start at 0, and they can be sliced, concatenated, and so on.

Accessing Values in Tuples

To access values in tuple, use the square brackets for slicing along with the index or indices to obtain value available at that index. For example –

```
#!/usr/bin/python
```

```
tup1 = ('physics', 'chemistry', 1997, 2000);

tup2 = (1, 2, 3, 4, 5, 6, 7 );

print "tup1[0]: ", tup1[0];

print "tup2[1:5]: ", tup2[1:5];
```

When the above code is executed, it produces the following result –

```
tup1[0]:  physics
tup2[1:5]:  [2, 3, 4, 5]
```

Updating Tuples:

Tuples are immutable which means you cannot update or change the values of tuple elements. You are able to take portions of existing tuples to create new tuples as the following example demonstrates –

```
#!/usr/bin/python
```

```
tup1 = (12, 34.56);

tup2 = ('abc', 'xyz');
```

```
# Following action is not valid for tuples

# tup1[0] = 100;


# So let's create a new tuple as follows

tup3 = tup1 + tup2;

print tup3;
```

When the above code is executed, it produces the following result −

```
(12, 34.56, 'abc', 'xyz')
```

Delete Tuple Elements:

Removing individual tuple elements is not possible. There is, of course, nothing wrong with putting together another tuple with the undesired elements discarded.

To explicitly remove an entire tuple, just use the **del** statement. For example −

```
#!/usr/bin/python


tup = ('physics', 'chemistry', 1997, 2000);

print tup;
```

```
del tup;

print "After deleting tup : ";

print tup;
```

This produces the following result. Note an exception raised, this is because after **del tup** tuple does not exist any more −

```
('physics', 'chemistry', 1997, 2000)
After deleting tup :
Traceback (most recent call last):
  File "test.py", line 9, in <module>
    print tup;
NameError: name 'tup' is not defined
```

Basic Tuples Operations:

Tuples respond to the + and * operators much like strings; they mean concatenation and repetition here too, except that the result is a new tuple, not a string.

In fact, tuples respond to all of the general sequence operations we used on strings in the prior chapter −

Python Expression	Results	Description
len((1, 2, 3))	3	Length

(1, 2, 3) + (4, 5, 6)	(1, 2, 3, 4, 5, 6)	Concatenation
('Hi!',) * 4	('Hi!', 'Hi!', 'Hi!', 'Hi!')	Repetition
3 in (1, 2, 3)	True	Membership
for x in (1, 2, 3): print x,	1 2 3	Iteration

Indexing, Slicing, and Matrixes:

Because tuples are sequences, indexing and slicing work the same way for tuples as they do for strings. Assuming following input −

```
L = ('spam', 'Spam', 'SPAM!')
```

Python Expression	Results	Description
L[2]	'SPAM!'	Offsets start at zero

| L[-2] | 'Spam' | Negative: count from the right |
| L[1:] | ['Spam', 'SPAM!'] | Slicing fetches sections |

No Enclosing Delimiters:

Any set of multiple objects, comma-separated, written without identifying symbols, i.e., brackets for lists, parentheses for tuples, etc., default to tuples, as indicated in these short examples −

```
#!/usr/bin/python


print 'abc', -4.24e93, 18+6.6j, 'xyz';

x, y = 1, 2;

print "Value of x , y : ", x,y;
```

When the above code is executed, it produces the following result −

```
abc -4.24e+93 (18+6.6j) xyz
Value of x , y : 1 2
```

Built-in Tuple Functions:

Python includes the following tuple functions −

Sr.No.	Function with Description
1	**cmp(tuple1, tuple2)** Compares elements of both tuples.
2	**len(tuple)** Gives the total length of the tuple.
3	**max(tuple)** Returns item from the tuple with max value.
4	**min(tuple)** Returns item from the tuple with min value.
5	**tuple(seq)** Converts a list into tuple.

Python – Dictionary

Each key is separated from its value by a colon (:), the items are separated by commas, and the whole thing is enclosed in curly braces. An empty dictionary without any items is written with just two curly braces, like this: {}.

Keys are unique within a dictionary while values may not be. The values of a dictionary can be of any type, but the keys must be of an immutable data type such as strings, numbers, or tuples.

Accessing Values in Dictionary:

To access dictionary elements, you can use the familiar square brackets along with the key to obtain its value. Following is a simple example –

```
#!/usr/bin/python


dict = {'Name': 'Zara', 'Age': 7, 'Class': 'First'}

print "dict['Name']: ", dict['Name']

print "dict['Age']: ", dict['Age']
```

When the above code is executed, it produces the following result –

```
dict['Name']:  Zara
dict['Age']:  7
```

If we attempt to access a data item with a key, which is not part of the dictionary, we get an error as follows −

```
#!/usr/bin/python


dict = {'Name': 'Zara', 'Age': 7, 'Class': 'First'}

print "dict['Alice']: ", dict['Alice']
```

When the above code is executed, it produces the following result −

```
dict['Alice']:
Traceback (most recent call last):
  File "test.py", line 4, in <module>
    print "dict['Alice']: ", dict['Alice'];
KeyError: 'Alice'
```

Updating Dictionary:

You can update a dictionary by adding a new entry or a key-value pair, modifying an existing entry, or deleting an existing entry as shown below in the simple example −

```
#!/usr/bin/python


dict = {'Name': 'Zara', 'Age': 7, 'Class': 'First'}

dict['Age'] = 8; # update existing entry
```

```
dict['School'] = "DPS School"; # Add new entry


print "dict['Age']: ", dict['Age']

print "dict['School']: ", dict['School']
```

When the above code is executed, it produces the following result –

```
dict['Age']:  8
dict['School']:  DPS School
```

Delete Dictionary Elements:

You can either remove individual dictionary elements or clear the entire contents of a dictionary. You can also delete entire dictionary in a single operation.

To explicitly remove an entire dictionary, just use the **del** statement. Following is a simple example –

```
#!/usr/bin/python


dict = {'Name': 'Zara', 'Age': 7, 'Class': 'First'}

del dict['Name']; # remove entry with key 'Name'

dict.clear();    # remove all entries in dict

del dict ;      # delete entire dictionary
```

```
print "dict['Age']: ", dict['Age']

print "dict['School']: ", dict['School']
```

This produces the following result. Note that an exception is raised because after **del dict** dictionary does not exist any more –

```
dict['Age']:
Traceback (most recent call last):
  File "test.py", line 8, in <module>
    print "dict['Age']: ", dict['Age'];
TypeError: 'type' object is unsubscriptable
```

Note – del() method is discussed in subsequent section.

Properties of Dictionary Keys:

Dictionary values have no restrictions. They can be any arbitrary Python object, either standard objects or user-defined objects. However, same is not true for the keys.

There are two important points to remember about dictionary keys –

(a) More than one entry per key not allowed. Which means no duplicate key is allowed. When duplicate keys encountered during assignment, the last assignment wins. For example –

```
#!/usr/bin/python


dict = {'Name': 'Zara', 'Age': 7, 'Name': 'Manni'}

print "dict['Name']: ", dict['Name']
```

When the above code is executed, it produces the following result −

```
dict['Name']:  Manni
```

(b) Keys must be immutable. Which means you can use strings, numbers or tuples as dictionary keys but something like ['key'] is not allowed. Following is a simple example −

```
#!/usr/bin/python


dict = {['Name']: 'Zara', 'Age': 7}

print "dict['Name']: ", dict['Name']
```

When the above code is executed, it produces the following result −

```
Traceback (most recent call last):
  File "test.py", line 3, in <module>
    dict = {['Name']: 'Zara', 'Age': 7};
TypeError: unhashable type: 'list'
```

Built-in Dictionary Functions & Methods:

Python includes the following dictionary functions −

Sr.No.	Function with Description
1	**cmp(dict1, dict2)** Compares elements of both dict.
2	**len(dict)** Gives the total length of the dictionary. This would be equal to the number of items in the dictionary.
3	**str(dict)** Produces a printable string representation of a dictionary
4	**type(variable)** Returns the type of the passed variable. If passed variable is dictionary, then it would return a dictionary type.

Python includes following dictionary methods –

Sr.No.	Methods with Description
1	**dict.clear()** Removes all elements of dictionary *dict*
2	**dict.copy()** Returns a shallow copy of dictionary *dict*
3	**dict.fromkeys()** Create a new dictionary with keys from seq and values *set* to *value.*
4	**dict.get(key, default=None)** For *key* key, returns value or default if key not in dictionary
5	**dict.has_key(key)** Returns *true* if key in dictionary *dict, false* otherwise
6	**dict.items()**

	Returns a list of *dict*'s (key, value) tuple pairs
7	**dict.keys()** Returns list of dictionary dict's keys
8	**dict.setdefault(key, default=None)** Similar to get(), but will set dict[key]=default if *key* is not already in dict
9	**dict.update(dict2)** Adds dictionary *dict2*'s key-values pairs to *dict*
10	**dict.values()** Returns list of dictionary *dict*'s values

Python - Date & Time

A Python program can handle date and time in several ways. Converting between date formats is a common chore for computers. Python's time and calendar modules help track dates and times.

What is Tick?

Time intervals are floating-point numbers in units of seconds. Particular instants in time are expressed in seconds since 12:00am, January 1, 1970(epoch).

There is a popular **time** module available in Python which provides functions for working with times, and for converting between representations. The function *time.time()* returns the current system time in ticks since 12:00am, January 1, 1970(epoch).

Example:

```
#!/usr/bin/python

import time;  # This is required to include time module.


ticks = time.time()

print "Number of ticks since 12:00am, January 1, 1970:", ticks
```

This would produce a result something as follows −

Number of ticks since 12:00am, January 1, 1970:
7186862.73399

Date arithmetic is easy to do with ticks. However, dates before the epoch cannot be represented in this form. Dates in the far future also cannot be represented this way - the cutoff point is sometime in 2038 for UNIX and Windows.

What is TimeTuple?

Many of Python's time functions handle time as a tuple of 9 numbers, as shown below –

Index	Field	Values
0	4-digit year	2008
1	Month	1 to 12
2	Day	1 to 31
3	Hour	0 to 23
4	Minute	0 to 59

5	Second	0 to 61 (60 or 61 are leap-seconds)
6	Day of Week	0 to 6 (0 is Monday)
7	Day of year	1 to 366 (Julian day)
8	Daylight savings	-1, 0, 1, -1 means library determines DST

The above tuple is equivalent to **struct_time** structure. This structure has following attributes –

Index	Attributes	Values
0	tm_year	2008
1	tm_mon	1 to 12
2	tm_mday	1 to 31
3	tm_hour	0 to 23

4	tm_min	0 to 59
5	tm_sec	0 to 61 (60 or 61 are leap-seconds)
6	tm_wday	0 to 6 (0 is Monday)
7	tm_yday	1 to 366 (Julian day)
8	tm_isdst	-1, 0, 1, -1 means library determines DST

Getting current time:

To translate a time instant from a *seconds since the epoch*floating-point value into a time-tuple, pass the floating-point value to a function (e.g., localtime) that returns a time-tuple with all nine items valid.

```
#!/usr/bin/python

import time;


localtime = time.localtime(time.time())
```

```
print "Local current time :", localtime
```

This would produce the following result, which could be formatted in any other presentable form –

```
Local current time : time.struct_time(tm_year=2013,
tm_mon=7,
tm_mday=17,   tm_hour=21,   tm_min=26,   tm_sec=3,
tm_wday=2, tm_yday=198, tm_isdst=0)
```

Getting formatted time:

You can format any time as per your requirement, but simple method to get time in readable format is asctime() –

```
#!/usr/bin/python

import time;


localtime = time.asctime( time.localtime(time.time()) )

print "Local current time :", localtime
```

This would produce the following result –

```
Local current time : Tue Jan 13 10:17:09 2009
```

Getting calendar for a month:

The calendar module gives a wide range of methods to play with yearly and monthly calendars. Here, we print a calendar for a given month (Jan 2008) –

```
#!/usr/bin/python

import calendar


cal = calendar.month(2008, 1)

print "Here is the calendar:"

print cal
```

This would produce the following result –

```
Here is the calendar:
     January 2008
Mo Tu We Th Fr Sa Su
    1  2  3  4  5  6
 7  8  9 10 11 12 13
14 15 16 17 18 19 20
21 22 23 24 25 26 27
28 29 30 31
```

The time Module:

There is a popular **time** module available in Python which provides functions for working with times and for converting between representations. Here is the list of all available methods −

Sr.No.	Function with Description
1	**time.altzone** The offset of the local DST timezone, in seconds west of UTC, if one is defined. This is negative if the local DST timezone is east of UTC (as in Western Europe, including the UK). Only use this if daylight is nonzero.
2	**time.asctime([tupletime])** Accepts a time-tuple and returns a readable 24-character string such as 'Tue Dec 11 18:07:14 2008'.
3	**time.clock( )** Returns the current CPU time as a floating-point number of seconds. To measure computational costs of different approaches, the value of

	time.clock is more useful than that of time.time().
4	**time.ctime([secs])** Like asctime(localtime(secs)) and without arguments is like asctime( )
5	**time.gmtime([secs])** Accepts an instant expressed in seconds since the epoch and returns a time-tuple t with the UTC time. Note : t.tm_isdst is always 0
6	**time.localtime([secs])** Accepts an instant expressed in seconds since the epoch and returns a time-tuple t with the local time (t.tm_isdst is 0 or 1, depending on whether DST applies to instant secs by local rules).
7	**time.mktime(tupletime)** Accepts an instant expressed as a time-tuple in local time and returns a floating-point value with the instant expressed in seconds since the epoch.

8	**time.sleep(secs)**
	Suspends the calling thread for secs seconds.
9	**time.strftime(fmt[,tupletime])**
	Accepts an instant expressed as a time-tuple in local time and returns a string representing the instant as specified by string fmt.
10	**time.strptime(str,fmt='%a %b %d %H:%M:%S %Y')**
	Parses str according to format string fmt and returns the instant in time-tuple format.
11	**time.time( )**
	Returns the current time instant, a floating-point number of seconds since the epoch.
12	**time.tzset()**
	Resets the time conversion rules used by the library routines. The environment variable TZ specifies how this is done.

Let us go through the functions briefly –

There are following two important attributes available with time module –

Sr.No.	Attribute with Description
1	**time.timezone** Attribute time.timezone is the offset in seconds of the local time zone (without DST) from UTC (>0 in the Americas; <=0 in most of Europe, Asia, Africa).
2	**time.tzname** Attribute time.tzname is a pair of locale-dependent strings, which are the names of the local time zone without and with DST, respectively.

The *calendar* Module:

The calendar module supplies calendar-related functions, including functions to print a text calendar for a given month or year.

By default, calendar takes Monday as the first day of the week and Sunday as the last one. To change this, call calendar.setfirstweekday() function.

Here is a list of functions available with the *calendar* module –

Sr.No.	Function with Description
1	**calendar.calendar(year,w=2,l=1,c=6)** Returns a multiline string with a calendar for year year formatted into three columns separated by c spaces. w is the width in characters of each date; each line has length 21*w+18+2*c. l is the number of lines for each week.
2	**calendar.firstweekday( )** Returns the current setting for the weekday that starts each week. By default, when calendar is first imported, this is 0, meaning Monday.
3	**calendar.isleap(year)** Returns True if year is a leap year; otherwise, False.

4	**calendar.leapdays(y1,y2)** Returns the total number of leap days in the years within range(y1,y2).
5	**calendar.month(year,month,w=2,l=1)** Returns a multiline string with a calendar for month month of year year, one line per week plus two header lines. w is the width in characters of each date; each line has length 7*w+6. l is the number of lines for each week.
6	**calendar.monthcalendar(year,month)** Returns a list of lists of ints. Each sublist denotes a week. Days outside month month of year year are set to 0; days within the month are set to their day-of-month, 1 and up.
7	**calendar.monthrange(year,month)** Returns two integers. The first one is the code of the weekday for the first day of the month month in year year; the second one is the number of days in the month. Weekday codes are 0 (Monday) to 6 (Sunday); month numbers are 1 to 12.

8	**calendar.prcal(year,w=2,l=1,c=6)**
	Like print calendar.calendar(year,w,l,c).
9	**calendar.prmonth(year,month,w=2,l=1)**
	Like print calendar.month(year,month,w,l).
10	**calendar.setfirstweekday(weekday)**
	Sets the first day of each week to weekday code weekday. Weekday codes are 0 (Monday) to 6 (Sunday).
11	**calendar.timegm(tupletime)**
	The inverse of time.gmtime: accepts a time instant in time-tuple form and returns the same instant as a floating-point number of seconds since the epoch.
12	**calendar.weekday(year,month,day)**
	Returns the weekday code for the given date. Weekday codes are 0 (Monday) to 6 (Sunday); month numbers are 1 (January) to 12 (December).

Other Modules & Functions:

If you are interested, then here you would find a list of other important modules and functions to play with date & time in Python –

- The *datetime* Module

- The *pytz* Module

- The *dateutil* Module

Python – Functions

A function is a block of organized, reusable code that is used to perform a single, related action. Functions provide better modularity for your application and a high degree of code reusing.

As you already know, Python gives you many built-in functions like print(), etc. but you can also create your own functions. These functions are called *user-defined functions*.

Defining a Function:

You can define functions to provide the required functionality. Here are simple rules to define a function in Python.

- Function blocks begin with the keyword **def** followed by the function name and parentheses (( )).

- Any input parameters or arguments should be placed within these parentheses. You can also define parameters inside these parentheses.

- The first statement of a function can be an optional statement - the documentation string of the function or *docstring*.

- The code block within every function starts with a colon (:) and is indented.

- The statement return [expression] exits a function, optionally passing back an expression to the caller. A return statement with no arguments is the same as return None.

Syntax

```
def functionname( parameters ):
  "function_docstring"
  function_suite
  return [expression]
```

By default, parameters have a positional behavior and you need to inform them in the same order that they were defined.

Example

The following function takes a string as input parameter and prints it on standard screen.

```
def printme( str ):

  "This prints a passed string into this function"

  print str

  return
```

Calling a Function:

Defining a function only gives it a name, specifies the parameters that are to be included in the function and structures the blocks of code.

Once the basic structure of a function is finalized, you can execute it by calling it from another function or directly from the Python prompt. Following is the example to call printme() function −

```
#!/usr/bin/python


# Function definition is here
def printme( str ):
   "This prints a passed string into this function"
   print str
   return;


# Now you can call printme function
printme("I'm first call to user defined function!")
printme("Again second call to the same function")
```

When the above code is executed, it produces the following result –

```
I'm first call to user defined function!
Again second call to the same function
```

Pass by reference vs value

All parameters (arguments) in the Python language are passed by reference. It means if you change what a parameter refers to within a function, the change also reflects back in the calling function. For example –

```python
#!/usr/bin/python


# Function definition is here
def changeme( mylist ):
   "This changes a passed list into this function"
   mylist.append([1,2,3,4]);
   print "Values inside the function: ", mylist
   return


# Now you can call changeme function
mylist = [10,20,30];
```

```
changeme( mylist );

print "Values outside the function: ", mylist
```

Here, we are maintaining reference of the passed object and appending values in the same object. So, this would produce the following result −

```
Values inside the function:  [10, 20, 30, [1, 2, 3, 4]]
Values outside the function:  [10, 20, 30, [1, 2, 3, 4]]
```

There is one more example where argument is being passed by reference and the reference is being overwritten inside the called function.

```
#!/usr/bin/python


# Function definition is here

def changeme( mylist ):

   "This changes a passed list into this function"

   mylist = [1,2,3,4]; # This would assig new reference in mylist

   print "Values inside the function: ", mylist

   return


# Now you can call changeme function
```

```
mylist = [10,20,30];

changeme( mylist );

print "Values outside the function: ", mylist
```

The parameter *mylist* is local to the function changeme. Changing mylist within the function does not affect *mylist*. The function accomplishes nothing and finally this would produce the following result –

```
Values inside the function:  [1, 2, 3, 4]
Values outside the function:  [10, 20, 30]
```

Function Arguments:

You can call a function by using the following types of formal arguments –

- Required arguments
- Keyword arguments
- Default arguments
- Variable-length arguments

Required arguments

Required arguments are the arguments passed to a function in correct positional order. Here, the number of arguments in the function call should match exactly with the function definition.

To call the function *printme()*, you definitely need to pass one argument, otherwise it gives a syntax error as follows –

```
#!/usr/bin/python


# Function definition is here

def printme( str ):

   "This prints a passed string into this function"

   print str

   return;


# Now you can call printme function

printme()
```

When the above code is executed, it produces the following result –

Traceback (most recent call last):

```
File "test.py", line 11, in <module>
    printme();
TypeError: printme() takes exactly 1 argument (0 given)
```

Keyword arguments:

Keyword arguments are related to the function calls. When you use keyword arguments in a function call, the caller identifies the arguments by the parameter name.

This allows you to skip arguments or place them out of order because the Python interpreter is able to use the keywords provided to match the values with parameters. You can also make keyword calls to the *printme()* function in the following ways –

```
#!/usr/bin/python


# Function definition is here

def printme( str ):

   "This prints a passed string into this function"

   print str

   return;


# Now you can call printme function
```

```
printme( str = "My string")
```

When the above code is executed, it produces the following result −

```
My string
```

The following example gives more clear picture. Note that the order of parameters does not matter.

```
#!/usr/bin/python


# Function definition is here
def printinfo( name, age ):
   "This prints a passed info into this function"
   print "Name: ", name
   print "Age ", age
   return;


# Now you can call printinfo function
printinfo( age=50, name="miki" )
```

When the above code is executed, it produces the following result −

```
Name:  miki
Age  50
```

Default arguments:

A default argument is an argument that assumes a default value if a value is not provided in the function call for that argument. The following example gives an idea on default arguments, it prints default age if it is not passed −

```python
#!/usr/bin/python


# Function definition is here
def printinfo( name, age = 35 ):
   "This prints a passed info into this function"
   print "Name: ", name
   print "Age ", age
   return;


# Now you can call printinfo function
printinfo( age=50, name="miki" )
printinfo( name="miki" )
```

When the above code is executed, it produces the following result –

```
Name: miki
Age 50
Name: miki
Age 35
```

Variable-length arguments:

You may need to process a function for more arguments than you specified while defining the function. These arguments are called *variable-length* arguments and are not named in the function definition, unlike required and default arguments.

Syntax for a function with non-keyword variable arguments is this –

```
def functionname([formal_args,] *var_args_tuple ):
  "function_docstring"
  function_suite
  return [expression]
```

An asterisk (*) is placed before the variable name that holds the values of all nonkeyword variable arguments. This tuple remains empty if no additional arguments are specified during the function call. Following is a simple example –

```
#!/usr/bin/python

# Function definition is here

def printinfo( arg1, *vartuple ):

   "This prints a variable passed arguments"

   print "Output is: "

   print arg1

   for var in vartuple:

      print var

   return;


# Now you can call printinfo function

printinfo( 10 )

printinfo( 70, 60, 50 )
```

When the above code is executed, it produces the following result −

```
Output is:
10
Output is:
70
60
50
```

The *Anonymous* Functions:

These functions are called anonymous because they are not declared in the standard manner by using the *def* keyword. You can use the *lambda* keyword to create small anonymous functions.

- Lambda forms can take any number of arguments but return just one value in the form of an expression. They cannot contain commands or multiple expressions.

- An anonymous function cannot be a direct call to print because lambda requires an expression

- Lambda functions have their own local namespace and cannot access variables other than those in their parameter list and those in the global namespace.

- Although it appears that lambda's are a one-line version of a function, they are not equivalent to inline statements in C or C++, whose purpose is by passing function stack allocation during invocation for performance reasons.

Syntax

The syntax of *lambda* functions contains only a single statement, which is as follows −

```
lambda [arg1 [,arg2,.....argn]]:expression
```

Following is the example to show how *lambda* form of function works −

```
#!/usr/bin/python


# Function definition is here

sum = lambda arg1, arg2: arg1 + arg2;


# Now you can call sum as a function

print "Value of total : ", sum( 10, 20 )

print "Value of total : ", sum( 20, 20 )
```

When the above code is executed, it produces the following result −

```
Value of total :  30
Value of total :  40
```

The *return* Statement:

The statement return [expression] exits a function, optionally passing back an expression to the caller. A return statement with no arguments is the same as return None.

All the above examples are not returning any value. You can return a value from a function as follows −

```
#!/usr/bin/python


# Function definition is here

def sum( arg1, arg2 ):

    # Add both the parameters and return them."

    total = arg1 + arg2

    print "Inside the function : ", total

    return total;


# Now you can call sum function

total = sum( 10, 20 );

print "Outside the function : ", total
```

When the above code is executed, it produces the following result −

```
Inside the function :  30
Outside the function :  30
```

Python – Modules

A module allows you to logically organize your Python code. Grouping related code into a module makes the code easier to understand and use. A module is a Python object with arbitrarily named attributes that you can bind and reference.

Simply, a module is a file consisting of Python code. A module can define functions, classes and variables. A module can also include runnable code.

Example

The Python code for a module named *aname* normally resides in a file named *aname.py*. Here's an example of a simple module, support.py

```
def print_func( par ):
  print "Hello : ", par
  return
```

The *import* Statement:

You can use any Python source file as a module by executing an import statement in some other Python source file. The *import* has the following syntax –

```
import module1[, module2[,... moduleN]
```

When the interpreter encounters an import statement, it imports the module if the module is present in the search path. A search path is a list of directories that the interpreter searches before importing a module. For example, to import the module support.py, you need to put the following command at the top of the script –

```
#!/usr/bin/python

# Import module support

import support

# Now you can call defined function that module as follows

support.print_func("Zara")
```

When the above code is executed, it produces the following result –

```
Hello : Zara
```

A module is loaded only once, regardless of the number of times it is imported. This prevents the module execution from happening over and over again if multiple imports occur.

The *from...import* Statement:

Python's *from* statement lets you import specific attributes from a module into the current namespace. The *from...import* has the following syntax −

```
from modname import name1[, name2[, ... nameN]]
```

For example, to import the function fibonacci from the module fib, use the following statement −

```
from fib import fibonacci
```

This statement does not import the entire module fib into the current namespace; it just introduces the item fibonacci from the module fib into the global symbol table of the importing module.

The *from...import* * Statement:

It is also possible to import all names from a module into the current namespace by using the following import statement −

```
from modname import *
```

This provides an easy way to import all the items from a module into the current namespace; however, this statement should be used sparingly.

Locating Modules:

When you import a module, the Python interpreter searches for the module in the following sequences –

- The current directory.

- If the module isn't found, Python then searches each directory in the shell variable PYTHONPATH.

- If all else fails, Python checks the default path. On UNIX, this default path is normally /usr/local/lib/python/.

The module search path is stored in the system module sys as the **sys.path** variable. The sys.path variable contains the current directory, PYTHONPATH, and the installation-dependent default.

The *PYTHONPATH* Variable:

The PYTHONPATH is an environment variable, consisting of a list of directories. The syntax of PYTHONPATH is the same as that of the shell variable PATH.

Here is a typical PYTHONPATH from a Windows system –

```
set PYTHONPATH = c:\python20\lib;
```

And here is a typical PYTHONPATH from a UNIX system –

```
set PYTHONPATH = /usr/local/lib/python
```

Namespaces and Scoping:

Variables are names (identifiers) that map to objects. A *namespace* is a dictionary of variable names (keys) and their corresponding objects (values).

A Python statement can access variables in a *local namespace* and in the *global namespace*. If a local and a global variable have the same name, the local variable shadows the global variable.

Each function has its own local namespace. Class methods follow the same scoping rule as ordinary functions.

Python makes educated guesses on whether variables are local or global. It assumes that any variable assigned a value in a function is local.

Therefore, in order to assign a value to a global variable within a function, you must first use the global statement.

The statement *global VarName* tells Python that VarName is a global variable. Python stops searching the local namespace for the variable.

For example, we define a variable *Money* in the global namespace. Within the function *Money*, we assign *Money* a value, therefore Python assumes *Money* as a local variable. However, we accessed the value of the local variable *Money*before setting it, so an UnboundLocalError is the result. Uncommenting the global statement fixes the problem.

```python
#!/usr/bin/python


Money = 2000
def AddMoney():
    # Uncomment the following line to fix the code:
    # global Money
    Money = Money + 1


print Money
AddMoney()
print Money
```

The dir( ) Function:

The dir() built-in function returns a sorted list of strings containing the names defined by a module.

The list contains the names of all the modules, variables and functions that are defined in a module. Following is a simple example –

```
#!/usr/bin/python


# Import built-in module math

import math


content = dir(math)

print content
```

When the above code is executed, it produces the following result –

```
['__doc__', '__file__', '__name__', 'acos', 'asin', 'atan',
'atan2', 'ceil', 'cos', 'cosh', 'degrees', 'e', 'exp',
'fabs', 'floor', 'fmod', 'frexp', 'hypot', 'ldexp', 'log',
'log10', 'modf', 'pi', 'pow', 'radians', 'sin', 'sinh',
'sqrt', 'tan', 'tanh']
```

Here, the special string variable __name__ is the module's name, and __file__ is the filename from which the module was loaded.

The *globals()* and *locals()* Functions:

The *globals()* and *locals()* functions can be used to return the names in the global and local namespaces depending on the location from where they are called.

If locals() is called from within a function, it will return all the names that can be accessed locally from that function.

If globals() is called from within a function, it will return all the names that can be accessed globally from that function.

The return type of both these functions is dictionary. Therefore, names can be extracted using the keys() function.

The *reload()* Function:

When the module is imported into a script, the code in the top-level portion of a module is executed only once.

Therefore, if you want to reexecute the top-level code in a module, you can use the *reload()* function. The reload() function imports a previously imported module again. The syntax of the reload() function is this −

```
reload(module_name)
```

Here, *module_name* is the name of the module you want to reload and not the string containing the module name. For example, to reload *hello* module, do the following –

```
reload(hello)
```

Packages in Python:

A package is a hierarchical file directory structure that defines a single Python application environment that consists of modules and subpackages and sub-subpackages, and so on.

Consider a file *Pots.py* available in *Phone* directory. This file has following line of source code –

```
#!/usr/bin/python


def Pots():
  print "I'm Pots Phone"
```

Similar way, we have another two files having different functions with the same name as above –

- *Phone/Isdn.py* file having function Isdn()

- *Phone/G3.py* file having function G3()

Now, create one more file __init__.py in *Phone* directory –

- Phone/__init__.py

To make all of your functions available when you've imported Phone, you need to put explicit import statements in __init__.py as follows –

```
from Pots import Pots
from Isdn import Isdn
from G3 import G3
```

After you add these lines to __init__.py, you have all of these classes available when you import the Phone package.

```
#!/usr/bin/python


# Now import your Phone Package.

import Phone


Phone.Pots()

Phone.Isdn()

Phone.G3()
```

When the above code is executed, it produces the following result –

```
I'm Pots Phone
I'm 3G Phone
I'm ISDN Phone
```

In the above example, we have taken example of a single functions in each file, but you can keep multiple functions in your files. You can also define different Python classes in those files and then you can create your packages out of those classes.

Python - Files I/O

This chapter covers all the basic I/O functions available in Python. For more functions, please refer to standard Python documentation.

Printing to the Screen

The simplest way to produce output is using the *print* statement where you can pass zero or more expressions separated by commas. This function converts the expressions you pass into a string and writes the result to standard output as follows –

```
#!/usr/bin/python


print "Python is really a great language,", "isn't it?"
```

This produces the following result on your standard screen –

```
Python is really a great language, isn't it?
```

Reading Keyboard Input:

Python provides two built-in functions to read a line of text from standard input, which by default comes from the keyboard. These functions are –

- raw_input
- input

The *raw_input* Function:

The *raw_input([prompt])* function reads one line from standard input and returns it as a string (removing the trailing newline).

```
#!/usr/bin/python


str = raw_input("Enter your input: ");

print "Received input is : ", str
```

This prompts you to enter any string and it would display same string on the screen. When I typed "Hello Python!", its output is like this −

```
Enter your input: Hello Python
Received input is :  Hello Python
```

The *input* Function:

The *input([prompt])* function is equivalent to raw_input, except that it assumes the input is a valid Python expression and returns the evaluated result to you.

```
#!/usr/bin/python


str = input("Enter your input: ");
```

```
print "Received input is : ", str
```

This would produce the following result against the entered input –

```
Enter your input: [x*5 for x in range(2,10,2)]
Recieved input is :  [10, 20, 30, 40]
```

Opening and Closing Files:

Until now, you have been reading and writing to the standard input and output. Now, we will see how to use actual data files.

Python provides basic functions and methods necessary to manipulate files by default. You can do most of the file manipulation using a **file** object.

The *open* Function:

Before you can read or write a file, you have to open it using Python's built-in *open()* function. This function creates a **file**object, which would be utilized to call other support methods associated with it.

Syntax

```
file object = open(file_name [, access_mode][, buffering])
```

Here are parameter details –

- **file_name** – The file_name argument is a string value that contains the name of the file that you want to access.

- **access_mode** – The access_mode determines the mode in which the file has to be opened, i.e., read, write, append, etc. A complete list of possible values is given below in the table. This is optional parameter and the default file access mode is read (r).

- **buffering** – If the buffering value is set to 0, no buffering takes place. If the buffering value is 1, line buffering is performed while accessing a file. If you specify the buffering value as an integer greater than 1, then buffering action is performed with the indicated buffer size. If negative, the buffer size is the system default(default behavior).

Here is a list of the different modes of opening a file –

Sr.No.	Modes & Description
1	**r** Opens a file for reading only. The file pointer is placed at the beginning of the file. This is the default mode.

2	**rb**
	Opens a file for reading only in binary format. The file pointer is placed at the beginning of the file. This is the default mode.
3	**r+**
	Opens a file for both reading and writing. The file pointer placed at the beginning of the file.
4	**rb+**
	Opens a file for both reading and writing in binary format. The file pointer placed at the beginning of the file.
5	**w**
	Opens a file for writing only. Overwrites the file if the file exists. If the file does not exist, creates a new file for writing.
6	**wb**
	Opens a file for writing only in binary format. Overwrites the file if the file exists. If the file does not exist, creates a new file for writing.

7	**w+** Opens a file for both writing and reading. Overwrites the existing file if the file exists. If the file does not exist, creates a new file for reading and writing.
8	**wb+** Opens a file for both writing and reading in binary format. Overwrites the existing file if the file exists. If the file does not exist, creates a new file for reading and writing.
9	**a** Opens a file for appending. The file pointer is at the end of the file if the file exists. That is, the file is in the append mode. If the file does not exist, it creates a new file for writing.
10	**ab** Opens a file for appending in binary format. The file pointer is at the end of the file if the file exists. That is, the file is in the append mode. If the file does not exist, it creates a new file for writing.

11	**a+** Opens a file for both appending and reading. The file pointer is at the end of the file if the file exists. The file opens in the append mode. If the file does not exist, it creates a new file for reading and writing.
12	**ab+** Opens a file for both appending and reading in binary format. The file pointer is at the end of the file if the file exists. The file opens in the append mode. If the file does not exist, it creates a new file for reading and writing.

The *file* Object Attributes

Once a file is opened and you have one *file* object, you can get various information related to that file.

Here is a list of all attributes related to file object −

Sr.No.	Attribute & Description
1	**file.closed**

	Returns true if file is closed, false otherwise.	
2	**file.mode** Returns access mode with which file was opened.	
3	**file.name** Returns name of the file.	
4	**file.softspace** Returns false if space explicitly required with print, true otherwise.	

Example:

```
#!/usr/bin/python


# Open a file

fo = open("foo.txt", "wb")

print "Name of the file: ", fo.name

print "Closed or not : ", fo.closed
```

```
print "Opening mode : ", fo.mode

print "Softspace flag : ", fo.softspace
```

This produces the following result −

```
Name of the file:  foo.txt
Closed or not :  False
Opening mode :  wb
Softspace flag :  0
```

The *close()* Method:

The close() method of a *file* object flushes any unwritten information and closes the file object, after which no more writing can be done.

Python automatically closes a file when the reference object of a file is reassigned to another file. It is a good practice to use the close() method to close a file.

Syntax

```
fileObject.close();
```

Example

```
#!/usr/bin/python



# Open a file
```

```
fo = open("foo.txt", "wb")

print "Name of the file: ", fo.name


# Close opend file

fo.close()
```

This produces the following result –

```
Name of the file:  foo.txt
```

Reading and Writing Files:

The *file* object provides a set of access methods to make our lives easier. We would see how to use *read()* and *write()* methods to read and write files.

The *write()* Method:

The *write()* method writes any string to an open file. It is important to note that Python strings can have binary data and not just text.

The write() method does not add a newline character ('\n') to the end of the string –

Syntax:

```
fileObject.write(string);
```

Here, passed parameter is the content to be written into the opened file.

Example:

```
#!/usr/bin/python


# Open a file

fo = open("foo.txt", "wb")

fo.write( "Python is a great language.\nYeah its great!!\n");


# Close opend file

fo.close()
```

The above method would create *foo.txt* file and would write given content in that file and finally it would close that file. If you would open this file, it would have following content.

```
Python is a great language.
Yeah its great!!
```

The *read()* Method:

The *read()* method reads a string from an open file. It is important to note that Python strings can have binary data. apart from text data.

Syntax

```
fileObject.read([count]);
```

Here, passed parameter is the number of bytes to be read from the opened file. This method starts reading from the beginning of the file and if *count* is missing, then it tries to read as much as possible, maybe until the end of file.

Example:

Let's take a file *foo.txt*, which we created above.

```
#!/usr/bin/python


# Open a file
fo = open("foo.txt", "r+")
str = fo.read(10);
print "Read String is : ", str
# Close opend file
fo.close()
```

This produces the following result –

Read String is : Python is

File Positions:

The *tell()* method tells you the current position within the file; in other words, the next read or write will occur at that many bytes from the beginning of the file.

The *seek(offset[, from])* method changes the current file position. The *offset* argument indicates the number of bytes to be moved. The *from* argument specifies the reference position from where the bytes are to be moved.

If *from* is set to 0, it means use the beginning of the file as the reference position and 1 means use the current position as the reference position and if it is set to 2 then the end of the file would be taken as the reference position.

Example:

Let us take a file *foo.txt*, which we created above.

```
#!/usr/bin/python


# Open a file

fo = open("foo.txt", "r+")

str = fo.read(10);

print "Read String is : ", str
```

```
# Check current position

position = fo.tell();

print "Current file position : ", position


# Reposition pointer at the beginning once again

position = fo.seek(0, 0);

str = fo.read(10);

print "Again read String is : ", str

# Close opend file

fo.close()
```

This produces the following result −

```
Read String is :  Python is
Current file position :  10
Again read String is :  Python is
```

Renaming and Deleting Files:

Python **os** module provides methods that help you perform file-processing operations, such as renaming and deleting files.

To use this module you need to import it first and then you can call any related functions.

The rename() Method:

The *rename()* method takes two arguments, the current filename and the new filename.

Syntax

```
os.rename(current_file_name, new_file_name)
```

Example

Following is the example to rename an existing file *test1.txt* −

```
#!/usr/bin/python

import os


# Rename a file from test1.txt to test2.txt

os.rename( "test1.txt", "test2.txt" )
```

The *remove()* Method:

You can use the *remove()* method to delete files by supplying the name of the file to be deleted as the argument.

Syntax:

```
os.remove(file_name)
```

Example:

Following is the example to delete an existing file *test2.txt* −

```
#!/usr/bin/python

import os


# Delete file test2.txt

os.remove("text2.txt")
```

Directories in Python:

All files are contained within various directories, and Python has no problem handling these too. The **os** module has several methods that help you create, remove, and change directories.

The *mkdir()* Method

You can use the *mkdir()* method of the **os** module to create directories in the current directory. You need to supply an argument to this method which contains the name of the directory to be created.

Syntax

```
os.mkdir("newdir")
```

Example

Following is the example to create a directory *test* in the current directory –

```
#!/usr/bin/python

import os


# Create a directory "test"

os.mkdir("test")
```

The *chdir()* Method

You can use the *chdir()* method to change the current directory. The chdir() method takes an argument, which is the name of the directory that you want to make the current directory.

Syntax

```
os.chdir("newdir")
```

Example

Following is the example to go into "/home/newdir" directory −

```
#!/usr/bin/python

import os


# Changing a directory to "/home/newdir"

os.chdir("/home/newdir")
```

The *getcwd()* Method

The *getcwd()* method displays the current working directory.

Syntax

```
os.getcwd()
```

Example

Following is the example to give current directory −

```
#!/usr/bin/python

import os
```

```
# This would give location of the current directory

os.getcwd()
```

The *rmdir()* Method

The *rmdir()* method deletes the directory, which is passed as an argument in the method.

Before removing a directory, all the contents in it should be removed.

Syntax

```
os.rmdir('dirname')
```

Example

Following is the example to remove "/tmp/test" directory. It is required to give fully qualified name of the directory, otherwise it would search for that directory in the current directory.

```
#!/usr/bin/python

import os


# This would remove "/tmp/test" directory.

os.rmdir( "/tmp/test" )
```

File & Directory Related Methods

There are three important sources, which provide a wide range of utility methods to handle and manipulate files & directories on Windows and Unix operating systems. They are as follows –

- File Object Methods: The *file* object provides functions to manipulate files.

- OS Object Methods: This provides methods to process files as well as directories.

Python - Exceptions Handling

Python provides two very important features to handle any unexpected error in your Python programs and to add debugging capabilities in them −

List of Standard Exceptions −

Sr.No.	Exception Name & Description
1	**Exception** Base class for all exceptions
2	**StopIteration** Raised when the next() method of an iterator does not point to any object.
3	**SystemExit** Raised by the sys.exit() function.
4	**StandardError** Base class for all built-in exceptions except StopIteration and SystemExit.
5	**ArithmeticError** Base class for all errors that occur for numeric

	calculation.
6	**OverflowError** Raised when a calculation exceeds maximum limit for a numeric type.
7	**FloatingPointError** Raised when a floating point calculation fails.
8	**ZeroDivisionError** Raised when division or modulo by zero takes place for all numeric types.
9	**AssertionError** Raised in case of failure of the Assert statement.
10	**AttributeError** Raised in case of failure of attribute reference or assignment.
11	**EOFError** Raised when there is no input from either the raw_input() or input() function and the end of

	file is reached.
12	**ImportError** Raised when an import statement fails.
13	**KeyboardInterrupt** Raised when the user interrupts program execution, usually by pressing Ctrl+c.
14	**LookupError** Base class for all lookup errors.
15	**IndexError** Raised when an index is not found in a sequence.
16	**KeyError** Raised when the specified key is not found in the dictionary.
17	**NameError** Raised when an identifier is not found in the local or global namespace.

18	**UnboundLocalError** Raised when trying to access a local variable in a function or method but no value has been assigned to it.
19	**EnvironmentError** Base class for all exceptions that occur outside the Python environment.
20	**IOError** Raised when an input/ output operation fails, such as the print statement or the open() function when trying to open a file that does not exist.
21	**IOError** Raised for operating system-related errors.
22	**SyntaxError** Raised when there is an error in Python syntax.
23	**IndentationError** Raised when indentation is not specified properly.

24	**SystemError**
	Raised when the interpreter finds an internal problem, but when this error is encountered the Python interpreter does not exit.
25	**SystemExit**
	Raised when Python interpreter is quit by using the sys.exit() function. If not handled in the code, causes the interpreter to exit.
26	**TypeError**
	Raised when an operation or function is attempted that is invalid for the specified data type.
27	**ValueError**
	Raised when the built-in function for a data type has the valid type of arguments, but the arguments have invalid values specified.
28	**RuntimeError**
	Raised when a generated error does not fall into any category.

29	**NotImplementedError**
	Raised when an abstract method that needs to be implemented in an inherited class is not actually implemented.

Assertions in Python:

An assertion is a sanity-check that you can turn on or turn off when you are done with your testing of the program.

The easiest way to think of an assertion is to liken it to a **raise-if**statement (or to be more accurate, a raise-if-not statement). An expression is tested, and if the result comes up false, an exception is raised.

Assertions are carried out by the assert statement, the newest keyword to Python, introduced in version 1.5.

Programmers often place assertions at the start of a function to check for valid input, and after a function call to check for valid output.

The *assert* Statement:

When it encounters an assert statement, Python evaluates the accompanying expression, which is hopefully true. If the expression is false, Python raises an *AssertionError* exception.

The syntax for assert is −

assert Expression[, Arguments]

If the assertion fails, Python uses ArgumentExpression as the argument for the AssertionError. AssertionError exceptions can be caught and handled like any other exception using the try-except statement, but if not handled, they will terminate the program and produce a traceback.

Example

Here is a function that converts a temperature from degrees Kelvin to degrees Fahrenheit. Since zero degrees Kelvin is as cold as it gets, the function bails out if it sees a negative temperature −

```
#!/usr/bin/python

def KelvinToFahrenheit(Temperature):
    assert (Temperature >= 0),"Colder than absolute zero!"
    return ((Temperature-273)*1.8)+32

print KelvinToFahrenheit(273)

print int(KelvinToFahrenheit(505.78))

print KelvinToFahrenheit(-5)
```

When the above code is executed, it produces the following result –

```
32.0
451
Traceback (most recent call last):
File "test.py", line 9, in <module>
print KelvinToFahrenheit(-5)
File "test.py", line 4, in KelvinToFahrenheit
assert (Temperature >= 0),"Colder than absolute zero!"
AssertionError: Colder than absolute zero!
```

What is Exception?:

An exception is an event, which occurs during the execution of a program that disrupts the normal flow of the program's instructions. In general, when a Python script encounters a situation that it cannot cope with, it raises an exception. An exception is a Python object that represents an error.

When a Python script raises an exception, it must either handle the exception immediately otherwise it terminates and quits.

Handling an exception:

If you have some *suspicious* code that may raise an exception, you can defend your program by placing the suspicious code in a **try:** block. After the try: block, include an **except:** statement, followed by a block of code which handles the problem as elegantly as possible.

Syntax

Here is simple syntax of *try....except...else* blocks –

```
try:
  You do your operations here;
  .....................
except ExceptionI:
  If there is ExceptionI, then execute this block.
except ExceptionII:
  If there is ExceptionII, then execute this block.
  .....................
else:
  If there is no exception then execute this block.
```

Here are few important points about the above-mentioned syntax –

- A single try statement can have multiple except statements. This is useful when the try block contains statements that may throw different types of exceptions.

- You can also provide a generic except clause, which handles any exception.

- After the except clause(s), you can include an else-clause. The code in the else-block executes if the code in the try: block does not raise an exception.

- The else-block is a good place for code that does not need the try: block's protection.

Example:

This example opens a file, writes content in the, file and comes out gracefully because there is no problem at all –

```
#!/usr/bin/python


try:

   fh = open("testfile", "w")

   fh.write("This is my test file for exception handling!!")

except IOError:

   print "Error: can\'t find file or read data"

else:

   print "Written content in the file successfully"

   fh.close()
```

This produces the following result –

```
Written content in the file successfully
```

Example

This example tries to open a file where you do not have write permission, so it raises an exception −

```
#!/usr/bin/python


try:

   fh = open("testfile", "r")

   fh.write("This is my test file for exception handling!!")
except IOError:

   print "Error: can\'t find file or read data"
else:

   print "Written content in the file successfully"
```

This produces the following result −

```
Error: can't find file or read data
```

The *except* Clause with No Exceptions

You can also use the except statement with no exceptions defined as follows −

```
try:
   You do your operations here;
   ....................
```

```
except:
    If there is any exception, then execute this block.
    ......................
else:
    If there is no exception then execute this block.
```

This kind of a **try-except** statement catches all the exceptions that occur. Using this kind of try-except statement is not considered a good programming practice though, because it catches all exceptions but does not make the programmer identify the root cause of the problem that may occur.

The *except* Clause with Multiple Exceptions:

You can also use the same *except* statement to handle multiple exceptions as follows −

```
try:

    You do your operations here;

    ......................

except(Exception1[, Exception2[,...ExceptionN]]):

    If there is any exception from the given exception list,

    then execute this block.

    ......................
```

else:

If there is no exception then execute this block.

The try-finally Clause:

You can use a **finally:** block along with a **try:** block. The finally block is a place to put any code that must execute, whether the try-block raised an exception or not. The syntax of the try-finally statement is this −

```
try:

    You do your operations here;

    ......................

    Due to any exception, this may be skipped.
finally:

    This would always be executed.

    ......................
```

You cannot use *else* clause as well along with a finally clause.

Example

```
#!/usr/bin/python
```

```
try:

   fh = open("testfile", "w")

   fh.write("This is my test file for exception handling!!")

finally:

   print "Error: can\'t find file or read data"
```

If you do not have permission to open the file in writing mode, then this will produce the following result −

```
Error: can't find file or read data
```

Same example can be written more cleanly as follows −

```
#!/usr/bin/python


try:

   fh = open("testfile", "w")

   try:

      fh.write("This is my test file for exception handling!!")

   finally:

      print "Going to close the file"

      fh.close()

except IOError:
```

```
print "Error: can\'t find file or read data"
```

When an exception is thrown in the *try* block, the execution immediately passes to the *finally* block. After all the statements in the *finally* block are executed, the exception is raised again and is handled in the *except* statements if present in the next higher layer of the *try-except* statement.

Argument of an Exception:

An exception can have an *argument*, which is a value that gives additional information about the problem. The contents of the argument vary by exception. You capture an exception's argument by supplying a variable in the except clause as follows −

```
try:

   You do your operations here;

   ......................

except ExceptionType, Argument:

   You can print value of Argument here...
```

If you write the code to handle a single exception, you can have a variable follow the name of the exception in the except statement. If you are trapping multiple exceptions, you can have a variable follow the tuple of the exception.

This variable receives the value of the exception mostly containing the cause of the exception. The variable can receive a single value or multiple values in the form of a tuple. This tuple usually contains the error string, the error number, and an error location.

Example:

Following is an example for a single exception −

```
#!/usr/bin/python


# Define a function here.

def temp_convert(var):

    try:

        return int(var)

    except ValueError, Argument:

        print "The argument does not contain numbers\n",
Argument


# Call above function here.

temp_convert("xyz");
```

This produces the following result −

```
The argument does not contain numbers
invalid literal for int() with base 10: 'xyz'
```

Raising an Exceptions:

You can raise exceptions in several ways by using the raise statement. The general syntax for the **raise** statement is as follows.

Syntax

```
raise [Exception [, args [, traceback]]]
```

Here, *Exception* is the type of exception (for example, NameError) and *argument* is a value for the exception argument. The argument is optional; if not supplied, the exception argument is None.

The final argument, traceback, is also optional (and rarely used in practice), and if present, is the traceback object used for the exception.

Example

An exception can be a string, a class or an object. Most of the exceptions that the Python core raises are classes, with an argument that is an instance of the class. Defining new exceptions is quite easy and can be done as follows −

```
def functionName( level ):
```

```
if level < 1:

    raise "Invalid level!", level

    # The code below to this would not be executed

    # if we raise the exception
```

Note: In order to catch an exception, an "except" clause must refer to the same exception thrown either class object or simple string. For example, to capture above exception, we must write the except clause as follows –

```
try:

    Business Logic here...

except "Invalid level!":

    Exception handling here...

else:

    Rest of the code here...
```

User-Defined Exceptions:

Python also allows you to create your own exceptions by deriving classes from the standard built-in exceptions.

Here is an example related to *RuntimeError*. Here, a class is created that is subclassed from *RuntimeError*. This is useful when you need to display more specific information when an exception is caught.

In the try block, the user-defined exception is raised and caught in the except block. The variable e is used to create an instance of the class *Networkerror*.

```
class Networkerror(RuntimeError):

  def __init__(self, arg):

    self.args = arg
```

So once you defined above class, you can raise the exception as follows –

```
try:

  raise Networkerror("Bad hostname")

except Networkerror,e:

  print e.args
```

Python - Object Oriented

Python has been an object-oriented language since it existed. Because of this, creating and using classes and objects are downright easy. This chapter helps you become an expert in using Python's object-oriented programming support.

If you do not have any previous experience with object-oriented (OO) programming, you may want to consult an introductory course on it or at least a tutorial of some sort so that you have a grasp of the basic concepts.

However, here is small introduction of Object-Oriented Programming (OOP) to bring you at speed –

Overview of OOP Terminology

- **Class** – A user-defined prototype for an object that defines a set of attributes that characterize any object of the class. The attributes are data members (class variables and instance variables) and methods, accessed via dot notation.

- **Class variable** – A variable that is shared by all instances of a class. Class variables are defined within a class but outside any of the class's methods. Class variables are not used as frequently as instance variables are.

- **Data member** – A class variable or instance variable that holds data associated with a class and its objects.

- **Function overloading** – The assignment of more than one behavior to a particular function. The operation performed varies by the types of objects or arguments involved.

- **Instance variable** – A variable that is defined inside a method and belongs only to the current instance of a class.

- **Inheritance** – The transfer of the characteristics of a class to other classes that are derived from it.

- **Instance** – An individual object of a certain class. An object obj that belongs to a class Circle, for example, is an instance of the class Circle.

- **Instantiation** – The creation of an instance of a class.

- **Method** – A special kind of function that is defined in a class definition.

- **Object** – A unique instance of a data structure that's defined by its class. An object comprises both data members (class variables and instance variables) and methods.

- **Operator overloading** – The assignment of more than one function to a particular operator.

Creating Classes:

The *class* statement creates a new class definition. The name of the class immediately follows the keyword *class* followed by a colon as follows –

```
class ClassName:
   'Optional class documentation string'
   class_suite
```

- The class has a documentation string, which can be accessed via *ClassName.__doc__*.

- The *class_suite* consists of all the component statements defining class members, data attributes and functions.

Example

Following is the example of a simple Python class –

```
class Employee:

   'Common base class for all employees'

   empCount = 0


   def __init__(self, name, salary):

      self.name = name

      self.salary = salary

      Employee.empCount += 1
```

```
def displayCount(self):

    print "Total Employee %d" % Employee.empCount


def displayEmployee(self):

    print "Name : ", self.name, ", Salary: ", self.salary
```

- The variable *empCount* is a class variable whose value is shared among all instances of a this class. This can be accessed as *Employee.empCount* from inside the class or outside the class.

- The first method *__init__()* is a special method, which is called class constructor or initialization method that Python calls when you create a new instance of this class.

- You declare other class methods like normal functions with the exception that the first argument to each method is *self*. Python adds the *self* argument to the list for you; you do not need to include it when you call the methods.

Creating Instance Objects:

To create instances of a class, you call the class using class name and pass in whatever arguments its __*init*__ method accepts.

```
"This would create first object of Employee class"
emp1 = Employee("Zara", 2000)
"This would create second object of Employee class"
emp2 = Employee("Manni", 5000)
```

Accessing Attributes:

You access the object's attributes using the dot operator with object. Class variable would be accessed using class name as follows –

```
emp1.displayEmployee()
emp2.displayEmployee()
print "Total Employee %d" % Employee.empCount
```

Now, putting all the concepts together –

```
#!/usr/bin/python


class Employee:

   'Common base class for all employees'

   empCount = 0
```

```python
    def __init__(self, name, salary):
        self.name = name
        self.salary = salary
        Employee.empCount += 1


    def displayCount(self):
        print "Total Employee %d" % Employee.empCount


    def displayEmployee(self):
        print "Name : ", self.name,  ", Salary: ", self.salary


"This would create first object of Employee class"
emp1 = Employee("Zara", 2000)
"This would create second object of Employee class"
emp2 = Employee("Manni", 5000)
emp1.displayEmployee()
emp2.displayEmployee()
print "Total Employee %d" % Employee.empCount
```

When the above code is executed, it produces the following result –

```
Name : Zara ,Salary: 2000
Name : Manni ,Salary: 5000
Total Employee 2
```

You can add, remove, or modify attributes of classes and objects at any time –

```
emp1.age = 7  # Add an 'age' attribute.
emp1.age = 8  # Modify 'age' attribute.
del emp1.age  # Delete 'age' attribute.
```

Instead of using the normal statements to access attributes, you can use the following functions –

- The **getattr(obj, name[, default])** – to access the attribute of object.

- The **hasattr(obj,name)** – to check if an attribute exists or not.

- The **setattr(obj,name,value)** – to set an attribute. If attribute does not exist, then it would be created.

- The **delattr(obj, name)** – to delete an attribute.

```
hasattr(emp1, 'age')   # Returns true if 'age' attribute exists
getattr(emp1, 'age')   # Returns value of 'age' attribute
setattr(emp1, 'age', 8) # Set attribute 'age' at 8
delattr(empl, 'age')   # Delete attribute 'age'
```

Built-In Class Attributes:

Every Python class keeps following built-in attributes and they can be accessed using dot operator like any other attribute –

- **__dict__** – Dictionary containing the class's namespace.

- **__doc__** – Class documentation string or none, if undefined.

- **__name__** – Class name.

- **__module__** – Module name in which the class is defined. This attribute is "__main__" in interactive mode.

- **__bases__** – A possibly empty tuple containing the base classes, in the order of their occurrence in the base class list.

For the above class let us try to access all these attributes –

```
#!/usr/bin/python


class Employee:

   'Common base class for all employees'

   empCount = 0
```

```
def __init__(self, name, salary):

    self.name = name

    self.salary = salary

    Employee.empCount += 1


def displayCount(self):

    print "Total Employee %d" % Employee.empCount


def displayEmployee(self):

    print "Name : ", self.name,  ", Salary: ", self.salary


print "Employee.__doc__:", Employee.__doc__

print "Employee.__name__:", Employee.__name__

print "Employee.__module__:", Employee.__module__

print "Employee.__bases__:", Employee.__bases__

print "Employee.__dict__:", Employee.__dict__
```

When the above code is executed, it produces the following result −

Employee.__doc__ : Common base class for all employees
Employee.__name__ : Employee
Employee.__module__ : __main__
Employee.__bases__ : ()
Employee.__dict__ : {'__module__': '__main__',
'displayCount':
<function displayCount at 0xb7c84994>, 'empCount': 2,
'displayEmployee': <function displayEmployee at
0xb7c8441c>,
'__doc__': 'Common base class for all employees',
'__init__': <function __init__ at 0xb7c846bc>}

Destroying Objects (Garbage Collection):

Python deletes unneeded objects (built-in types or class instances) automatically to free the memory space. The process by which Python periodically reclaims blocks of memory that no longer are in use is termed Garbage Collection.

Python's garbage collector runs during program execution and is triggered when an object's reference count reaches zero. An object's reference count changes as the number of aliases that point to it changes.

An object's reference count increases when it is assigned a new name or placed in a container (list, tuple, or dictionary). The object's reference count decreases when it's deleted with *del*, its reference is reassigned, or its reference goes out of scope. When an object's reference count reaches zero, Python collects it automatically.

```
a = 40     # Create object <40>
b = a      # Increase ref. count of <40>
c = [b]    # Increase ref. count of <40>

del a      # Decrease ref. count of <40>
b = 100    # Decrease ref. count of <40>
c[0] = -1  # Decrease ref. count of <40>
```

You normally will not notice when the garbage collector destroys an orphaned instance and reclaims its space. But a class can implement the special method __del__(), called a destructor, that is invoked when the instance is about to be destroyed. This method might be used to clean up any non memory resources used by an instance.

Example:

This __del__() destructor prints the class name of an instance that is about to be destroyed −

```
#!/usr/bin/python


class Point:

 def __init__(self, x=0, y=0):

  self.x = x
```

```
    self.y = y
  def __del__(self):
    class_name = self.__class__.__name__
    print class_name, "destroyed"


pt1 = Point()

pt2 = pt1

pt3 = pt1

print id(pt1), id(pt2), id(pt3) # prints the ids of the obejcts

del pt1

del pt2

del pt3
```

When the above code is executed, it produces following result –

```
3083401324 3083401324 3083401324
Point destroyed
```

Note – Ideally, you should define your classes in separate file, then you should import them in your main program file using *import* statement.

Class Inheritance:

Instead of starting from scratch, you can create a class by deriving it from a preexisting class by listing the parent class in parentheses after the new class name.

The child class inherits the attributes of its parent class, and you can use those attributes as if they were defined in the child class. A child class can also override data members and methods from the parent.

Syntax

Derived classes are declared much like their parent class; however, a list of base classes to inherit from is given after the class name −

```
class SubClassName (ParentClass1[, ParentClass2, ...]):
   'Optional class documentation string'
   class_suite
```

Example

```
#!/usr/bin/python


class Parent:      # define parent class
   parentAttr = 100
   def __init__(self):
```

```python
    print "Calling parent constructor"

  def parentMethod(self):
    print 'Calling parent method'

  def setAttr(self, attr):
    Parent.parentAttr = attr

  def getAttr(self):
    print "Parent attribute :", Parent.parentAttr

class Child(Parent): # define child class
  def __init__(self):
    print "Calling child constructor"

  def childMethod(self):
    print 'Calling child method'

c = Child()        # instance of child
```

```
c.childMethod()     # child calls its method

c.parentMethod()    # calls parent's method

c.setAttr(200)      # again call parent's method

c.getAttr()         # again call parent's method
```

When the above code is executed, it produces the following result −

```
Calling child constructor
Calling child method
Calling parent method
Parent attribute : 200
```

Similar way, you can drive a class from multiple parent classes as follows −

```
class A:      # define your class A
.....

class B:      # define your class B
.....

class C(A, B):  # subclass of A and B
.....
```

You can use issubclass() or isinstance() functions to check a relationships of two classes and instances.

- The **issubclass(sub, sup)** boolean function returns true if the given subclass **sub** is indeed a subclass of the superclass **sup**.

- The **isinstance(obj,   Class)** boolean   function returns true if *obj* is an instance of class *Class* or is an instance of a subclass of Class

Overriding Methods:

You can always override your parent class methods. One reason for overriding parent's methods is because you may want special or different functionality in your subclass.

Example

```
#!/usr/bin/python


class Parent:      # define parent class
  def myMethod(self):
    print 'Calling parent method'


class Child(Parent): # define child class
  def myMethod(self):
    print 'Calling child method'
```

```
c = Child()        # instance of child

c.myMethod()       # child calls overridden method
```

When the above code is executed, it produces the following result −

```
Calling child method
```

Base Overloading Methods:

Following table lists some generic functionality that you can override in your own classes −

Sr.No.	Method, Description & Sample Call
1	**__init__ (self [,args...])** Constructor (with any optional arguments) Sample Call : *obj = className(args)*
2	**__del__(self)** Destructor, deletes an object Sample Call : *del obj*
3	**__repr__(self)**

	Evaluable string representation
	Sample Call : *repr(obj)*
4	**__str__(self)**
	Printable string representation
	Sample Call : *str(obj)*
5	**__cmp__ (self, x)**
	Object comparison
	Sample Call : *cmp(obj, x)*

Overloading Operators:

Suppose you have created a Vector class to represent two-dimensional vectors, what happens when you use the plus operator to add them? Most likely Python will yell at you.

You could, however, define the *__add__* method in your class to perform vector addition and then the plus operator would behave as per expectation –

Example

```
#!/usr/bin/python
```

```
class Vector:

  def __init__(self, a, b):

    self.a = a

    self.b = b


  def __str__(self):

    return 'Vector (%d, %d)' % (self.a, self.b)


  def __add__(self,other):

    return Vector(self.a + other.a, self.b + other.b)


v1 = Vector(2,10)

v2 = Vector(5,-2)

print v1 + v2
```

When the above code is executed, it produces the following result −

```
Vector(7,8)
```

Data Hiding:

An object's attributes may or may not be visible outside the class definition. You need to name attributes with a double underscore prefix, and those attributes then are not be directly visible to outsiders.

Example

```
#!/usr/bin/python


class JustCounter:

    __secretCount = 0


    def count(self):

        self.__secretCount += 1

        print self.__secretCount


counter = JustCounter()

counter.count()

counter.count()
```

```
print counter.__secretCount
```

When the above code is executed, it produces the following result −

```
1
2
Traceback (most recent call last):
  File "test.py", line 12, in <module>
    print counter.__secretCount
AttributeError: JustCounter instance has no attribute
'__secretCount'
```

Python protects those members by internally changing the name to include the class name. You can access such attributes as *object._className__attrName*. If you would replace your last line as following, then it works for you −

```
.......................
print counter._JustCounter__secretCount
```

When the above code is executed, it produces the following result −

```
1
2
2
```

Python - Regular Expressions

A *regular expression* is a special sequence of characters that helps you match or find other strings or sets of strings, using a specialized syntax held in a pattern. Regular expressions are widely used in UNIX world.

The module **re** provides full support for Perl-like regular expressions in Python. The re module raises the exception re.error if an error occurs while compiling or using a regular expression.

We would cover two important functions, which would be used to handle regular expressions. But a small thing first: There are various characters, which would have special meaning when they are used in regular expression. To avoid any confusion while dealing with regular expressions, we would use Raw Strings as **r'expression'**.

The *match* Function

This function attempts to match RE *pattern* to *string* with optional *flags*.

Here is the syntax for this function –

```
re.match(pattern, string, flags=0)
```

Here is the description of the parameters –

Sr.No.	Parameter & Description
1	**pattern** This is the regular expression to be matched.
2	**string** This is the string, which would be searched to match the pattern at the beginning of string.
3	**flags** You can specify different flags using bitwise OR (|). These are modifiers, which are listed in the table below.

The *re.match* function returns a **match** object on success, **None**on failure. We use*group(num)* or *groups()* function of **match**object to get matched expression.

Sr.No.	Match Object Method & Description
1	**group(num=0)**

	This method returns entire match (or specific subgroup num)
2	**groups()** This method returns all matching subgroups in a tuple (empty if there weren't any)

Example

```
#!/usr/bin/python

import re


line = "Cats are smarter than dogs"


matchObj = re.match( r'(.*) are (.*?) .*', line, re.M|re.I)


if matchObj:
   print "matchObj.group() : ", matchObj.group()
   print "matchObj.group(1) : ", matchObj.group(1)
   print "matchObj.group(2) : ", matchObj.group(2)
else:
```

```
print "No match!!"
```

When the above code is executed, it produces following result −

```
matchObj.group() :  Cats are smarter than dogs
matchObj.group(1) :  Cats
matchObj.group(2) :  smarter
```

The *search* Function:

This function searches for first occurrence of RE *pattern* within *string* with optional *flags*.

Here is the syntax for this function −

```
re.search(pattern, string, flags=0)
```

Here is the description of the parameters −

Sr.No.	Parameter & Description
1	**pattern** This is the regular expression to be matched.
2	**string** This is the string, which would be searched to match the pattern anywhere in the string.

3	flags
	You can specify different flags using bitwise OR (|). These are modifiers, which are listed in the table below.

The *re.search* function returns a **match** object on success, **none** on failure. We use *group(num)* or *groups()* function of **match** object to get matched expression.

Sr.No.	Match Object Methods & Description
1	**group(num=0)** This method returns entire match (or specific subgroup num)
2	**groups()** This method returns all matching subgroups in a tuple (empty if there weren't any)

Example

```
#!/usr/bin/python

import re


line = "Cats are smarter than dogs";


searchObj = re.search( r'(.*) are (.*?) .*', line, re.M|re.I)


if searchObj:
   print "searchObj.group() : ", searchObj.group()
   print "searchObj.group(1) : ", searchObj.group(1)
   print "searchObj.group(2) : ", searchObj.group(2)
else:
   print "Nothing found!!"
```

When the above code is executed, it produces following result −

```
searchObj.group() :  Cats are smarter than dogs
searchObj.group(1) :  Cats
searchObj.group(2) :  smarter
```

Matching Versus Searching:

Python offers two different primitive operations based on regular expressions: **match** checks for a match only at the beginning of the string, while **search** checks for a match anywhere in the string (this is what Perl does by default).

Example

```
#!/usr/bin/python

import re


line = "Cats are smarter than dogs";


matchObj = re.match( r'dogs', line, re.M|re.I)

if matchObj:

   print "match --> matchObj.group() : ", matchObj.group()

else:

   print "No match!!"


searchObj = re.search( r'dogs', line, re.M|re.I)

if searchObj:
```

```
  print "search --> searchObj.group() : ", searchObj.group()
else:
  print "Nothing found!!"
```

When the above code is executed, it produces the following result –

```
No match!!
search --> matchObj.group() :  dogs
```

Search and Replace:

One of the most important **re** methods that use regular expressions is **sub**.

Syntax

```
re.sub(pattern, repl, string, max=0)
```

This method replaces all occurrences of the RE *pattern* in *string*with *repl*, substituting all occurrences unless *max* provided. This method returns modified string.

Example

```
#!/usr/bin/python

import re


phone = "2004-959-559 # This is Phone Number"
```

```
# Delete Python-style comments

num = re.sub(r'#.*$', "", phone)

print "Phone Num : ", num


# Remove anything other than digits

num = re.sub(r'\D', "", phone)

print "Phone Num : ", num
```

When the above code is executed, it produces the following result −

```
Phone Num :  2004-959-559
Phone Num :  2004959559
```

Regular Expression Modifiers: Option Flags

Regular expression literals may include an optional modifier to control various aspects of matching. The modifiers are specified as an optional flag. You can provide multiple modifiers using exclusive OR (|), as shown previously and may be represented by one of these −

Sr.No.	Modifier & Description
1	**re.I** Performs case-insensitive matching.
2	**re.L** Interprets words according to the current locale. This interpretation affects the alphabetic group (\w and \W), as well as word boundary behavior(\b and \B).
3	**re.M** Makes $ match the end of a line (not just the end of the string) and makes ^ match the start of any line (not just the start of the string).
4	**re.S** Makes a period (dot) match any character, including a newline.
5	**re.U** Interprets letters according to the Unicode character set. This flag affects the behavior of \w,

	\W, \b, \B.
6	**re.X** Permits "cuter" regular expression syntax. It ignores whitespace (except inside a set [] or when escaped by a backslash) and treats unescaped # as a comment marker.

Regular Expression Patterns:

Except for control characters, (+ ? . * ^ $ ( ) [ ] { } | \), all characters match themselves. You can escape a control character by preceding it with a backslash.

Following table lists the regular expression syntax that is available in Python −

Sr.No.	Pattern & Description
1	^ Matches beginning of line.
2	$ Matches end of line.

3	. Matches any single character except newline. Using m option allows it to match newline as well.
4	**[...]** Matches any single character in brackets.
5	**[^...]** Matches any single character not in brackets
6	**re*** Matches 0 or more occurrences of preceding expression.
7	**re+** Matches 1 or more occurrence of preceding expression.
8	**re?** Matches 0 or 1 occurrence of preceding expression.

9	**re{ n}** Matches exactly n number of occurrences of preceding expression.
10	**re{ n,}** Matches n or more occurrences of preceding expression.
11	**re{ n, m}** Matches at least n and at most m occurrences of preceding expression.
12	**a| b** Matches either a or b.
13	**(re)** Groups regular expressions and remembers matched text.
14	**(?imx)** Temporarily toggles on i, m, or x options within a regular expression. If in parentheses, only that area is affected.

15	**(?-imx)**
	Temporarily toggles off i, m, or x options within a regular expression. If in parentheses, only that area is affected.
16	**(?: re)**
	Groups regular expressions without remembering matched text.
17	**(?imx: re)**
	Temporarily toggles on i, m, or x options within parentheses.
18	**(?-imx: re)**
	Temporarily toggles off i, m, or x options within parentheses.
19	**(?#...)**
	Comment.
20	**(?= re)**
	Specifies position using a pattern. Doesn't have a range.

21	**(?! re)** Specifies position using pattern negation. Doesn't have a range.
22	**(?> re)** Matches independent pattern without backtracking.
23	**\w** Matches word characters.
24	**\W** Matches nonword characters.
25	**\s** Matches whitespace. Equivalent to [\t\n\r\f].
26	**\S** Matches nonwhitespace.
27	**\d** Matches digits. Equivalent to [0-9].

28	\D Matches nondigits.
29	\A Matches beginning of string.
30	\Z Matches end of string. If a newline exists, it matches just before newline.
31	\z Matches end of string.
32	\G Matches point where last match finished.
33	\b Matches word boundaries when outside brackets. Matches backspace (0x08) when inside brackets.
34	\B Matches nonword boundaries.

35	**\n, \t, etc.**
	Matches newlines, carriage returns, tabs, etc.
36	**\1...\9**
	Matches nth grouped subexpression.
37	**\10**
	Matches nth grouped subexpression if it matched already. Otherwise refers to the octal representation of a character code.

Regular Expression Examples

Literal characters

Sr.No.	Example & Description
1	**python**
	Match "python".

Character classes:

Sr.No.	Example & Description
1	**[Pp]ython** Match "Python" or "python"
2	**rub[ye]** Match "ruby" or "rube"
3	**[aeiou]** Match any one lowercase vowel
4	**[0-9]** Match any digit; same as [0123456789]
5	**[a-z]** Match any lowercase ASCII letter
6	**[A-Z]** Match any uppercase ASCII letter

7	**[a-zA-Z0-9]** Match any of the above
8	**[^aeiou]** Match anything other than a lowercase vowel
9	**[^0-9]** Match anything other than a digit

Special Character Classes:

Sr.No.	Example & Description
1	. Match any character except newline
2	**\d** Match a digit: [0-9]
3	**\D**

	Match a nondigit: [^0-9]
4	**\s** Match a whitespace character: [\t\r\n\f]
5	**\S** Match nonwhitespace: [^ \t\r\n\f]
6	**\w** Match a single word character: [A-Za-z0-9_]
7	**\W** Match a nonword character: [^A-Za-z0-9_]

Repetition Cases:

Sr.No.	Example & Description
1	**ruby?** Match "rub" or "ruby": the y is optional

2	**ruby***
	Match "rub" plus 0 or more ys

3	**ruby+**
	Match "rub" plus 1 or more ys

4	**\d{3}**
	Match exactly 3 digits

5	**\d{3,}**
	Match 3 or more digits

6	**\d{3,5}**
	Match 3, 4, or 5 digits

Nongreedy repetition:

This matches the smallest number of repetitions −

Sr.No.	Example & Description
1	**<.*>**

	Greedy repetition: matches "\<python\>perl\>"
2	**\<.*?\>** Nongreedy: matches "\<python\>" in "\<python\>perl\>"

Grouping with Parentheses:

Sr.No.	Example & Description
1	**\D\d+** No group: + repeats \d
2	**(\D\d)+** Grouped: + repeats \D\d pair
3	**([Pp]ython(,)?)+** Match "Python", "Python, python, python", etc.

Backreferences:

This matches a previously matched group again –

Sr.No.	Example & Description
1	**([Pp])ython&\1ails** Match python&pails or Python&Pails
2	**(['"])[^\1]*\1** Single or double-quoted string. \1 matches whatever the 1st group matched. \2 matches whatever the 2nd group matched, etc.

Alternatives:

Sr.No.	Example & Description
1	**python|perl** Match "python" or "perl"
2	**rub(y|le))**

	Match "ruby" or "ruble"
3	**Python(!+|\?)** "Python" followed by one or more ! or one ?

Anchors:

This needs to specify match position.

Sr.No.	Example & Description
1	**^Python** Match "Python" at the start of a string or internal line
2	**Python$** Match "Python" at the end of a string or line
3	**\APython** Match "Python" at the start of a string
4	**Python\Z** Match "Python" at the end of a string

5	**\bPython\b**
	Match "Python" at a word boundary
6	**\brub\B**
	\B is nonword boundary: match "rub" in "rube" and "ruby" but not alone
7	**Python(?=!)**
	Match "Python", if followed by an exclamation point.
8	**Python(?!!)**
	Match "Python", if not followed by an exclamation point.

Special Syntax with Parentheses

Sr.No.	Example & Description
1	**R(?#comment)**
	Matches "R". All the rest is a comment

2	**R(?i)uby** Case-insensitive while matching "uby"
3	**R(?i:uby)** Same as above
4	**rub(?:y|le))** Group only without creating \1 backreference

Python - CGI Programming

The Common Gateway Interface, or CGI, is a set of standards that define how information is exchanged between the web server and a custom script. The CGI specs are currently maintained by the NCSA.

What is CGI?

- The Common Gateway Interface, or CGI, is a standard for external gateway programs to interface with information servers such as HTTP servers.

- The current version is CGI/1.1 and CGI/1.2 is under progress.

Web Browsing

To understand the concept of CGI, let us see what happens when we click a hyper link to browse a particular web page or URL.

- Your browser contacts the HTTP web server and demands for the URL, i.e., filename.

- Web Server parses the URL and looks for the filename. If it finds that file then sends it back to the browser, otherwise sends an error message indicating that you requested a wrong file.

- Web browser takes response from web server and displays either the received file or error message.

However, it is possible to set up the HTTP server so that whenever a file in a certain directory is requested that file is not sent back; instead it is executed as a program, and whatever that program outputs is sent back for your browser to display. This function is called the Common Gateway Interface or CGI and the programs are called CGI scripts. These CGI programs can be a Python Script, PERL Script, Shell Script, C or C++ program, etc.

CGI Architecture Diagram:

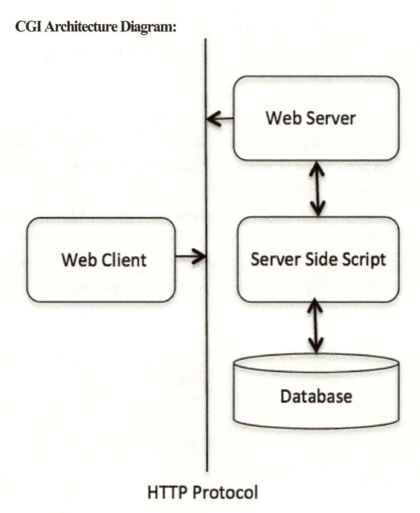

Web Server Support and Configuration:

Before you proceed with CGI Programming, make sure that your Web Server supports CGI and it is configured to handle CGI Programs. All the CGI Programs to be executed by the HTTP server are kept in a pre-configured directory. This directory is called CGI Directory and by convention it is named as /var/www/cgi-bin. By convention, CGI files have extension as. **cgi,** but you can keep your files with python extension **.py** as well.

By default, the Linux server is configured to run only the scripts in the cgi-bin directory in /var/www. If you want to specify any other directory to run your CGI scripts, comment the following lines in the httpd.conf file −

```
<Directory "/var/www/cgi-bin">

    AllowOverride None

    Options ExecCGI

    Order allow,deny

    Allow from all
</Directory>


<Directory "/var/www/cgi-bin">
Options All
</Directory>
```

Here, we assume that you have Web Server up and running successfully and you are able to run any other CGI program like Perl or Shell, etc.

First CGI Program:

Here is a simple link, which is linked to a CGI script called hello.py. This file is kept in /var/www/cgi-bin directory and it has following content. Before running your CGI program, make sure you have change mode of file using **chmod 755 hello.py**UNIX command to make file executable.

```
#!/usr/bin/python


print "Content-type:text/html\r\n\r\n"

print '<html>'

print '<head>'

print '<title>Hello Word - First CGI Program</title>'

print '</head>'

print '<body>'

print '<h2>Hello Word! This is my first CGI program</h2>'

print '</body>'

print '</html>'
```

If you click hello.py, then this produces the following output –

Hello Word! This is my first CGI program

This hello.py script is a simple Python script, which writes its output on STDOUT file, i.e., screen. There is one important and extra feature available which is first line to be printed **Content-type:text/html\r\n\r\n**. This line is sent back to the browser and it specifies the content type to be displayed on the browser screen.

By now you must have understood basic concept of CGI and you can write many complicated CGI programs using Python. This script can interact with any other external system also to exchange information such as RDBMS.

HTTP Header:

The line **Content-type:text/html\r\n\r\n** is part of HTTP header which is sent to the browser to understand the content. All the HTTP header will be in the following form −

HTTP Field Name: Field Content

For Example
Content-type: text/html\r\n\r\n

There are few other important HTTP headers, which you will use frequently in your CGI Programming.

Sr.No.	Header & Description
1	**Content-type:** A MIME string defining the format of the file being returned. Example is Content-type:text/html
2	**Expires: Date** The date the information becomes invalid. It is used by the browser to decide when a page needs to be refreshed. A valid date string is in the format 01 Jan 1998 12:00:00 GMT.
3	**Location: URL** The URL that is returned instead of the URL requested. You can use this field to redirect a request to any file.
4	**Last-modified: Date** The date of last modification of the resource.
5	**Content-length: N** The length, in bytes, of the data being returned.

	The browser uses this value to report the estimated download time for a file.
6	**Set-Cookie: String** Set the cookie passed through the *string*

CGI Environment Variables:

All the CGI programs have access to the following environment variables. These variables play an important role while writing any CGI program.

Sr.No.	Variable Name & Description
1	**CONTENT_TYPE** The data type of the content. Used when the client is sending attached content to the server. For example, file upload.
2	**CONTENT_LENGTH** The length of the query information. It is available only for POST requests.
3	**HTTP_COOKIE**

	Returns the set cookies in the form of key & value pair.
4	**HTTP_USER_AGENT** The User-Agent request-header field contains information about the user agent originating the request. It is name of the web browser.
5	**PATH_INFO** The path for the CGI script.
6	**QUERY_STRING** The URL-encoded information that is sent with GET method request.
7	**REMOTE_ADDR** The IP address of the remote host making the request. This is useful logging or for authentication.
8	**REMOTE_HOST** The fully qualified name of the host making the request. If this information is not available, then

	REMOTE_ADDR can be used to get IR address.
9	**REQUEST_METHOD** The method used to make the request. The most common methods are GET and POST.
10	**SCRIPT_FILENAME** The full path to the CGI script.
11	**SCRIPT_NAME** The name of the CGI script.
12	**SERVER_NAME** The server's hostname or IP Address
13	**SERVER_SOFTWARE** The name and version of the software the server is running.

Here is small CGI program to list out all the CGI variables.

```
#!/usr/bin/python

import os

print "Content-type: text/html\r\n\r\n";

print "<font size=+1>Environment</font><\br>";

for param in os.environ.keys():

   print    "<b>%20s</b>:    %s<\br>"    %    (param,
os.environ[param])
```

GET and POST Methods:

You must have come across many situations when you need to pass some information from your browser to web server and ultimately to your CGI Program. Most frequently, browser uses two methods two pass this information to web server. These methods are GET Method and POST Method.

Passing Information using GET method:

The GET method sends the encoded user information appended to the page request. The page and the encoded information are separated by the ? character as follows −

http://www.test.com/cgi-bin/hello.py?key1=value1&key2=value2

The GET method is the default method to pass information from browser to web server and it produces a long string that appears in your browser's Location:box. Never use GET method if you have password or other sensitive information to pass to the server. The GET method has size limitation: only 1024 characters can be sent in a request string. The GET method sends information using QUERY_STRING header and will be accessible in your CGI Program through QUERY_STRING environment variable.

You can pass information by simply concatenating key and value pairs along with any URL or you can use HTML <FORM> tags to pass information using GET method.

Simple URL Example: Get Method

Here is a simple URL, which passes two values to hello_get.py program using GET method.

/cgi-bin/hello_get.py?first_name=ZARA&last_name=ALI

Below is **hello_get.py** script to handle input given by web browser. We are going to use **cgi** module, which makes it very easy to access passed information −

```
#!/usr/bin/python


# Import modules for CGI handling

import cgi, cgitb


# Create instance of FieldStorage

form = cgi.FieldStorage()


# Get data from fields

first_name = form.getvalue('first_name')

last_name  = form.getvalue('last_name')


print "Content-type:text/html\r\n\r\n"

print "<html>"

print "<head>"

print "<title>Hello - Second CGI Program</title>"

print "</head>"

print "<body>"

print "<h2>Hello %s %s</h2>" % (first_name, last_name)
```

```
print "</body>"

print "</html>"
```

This would generate the following result −

```
Hello ZARA ALI
```

Simple FORM Example: GET Method

This example passes two values using HTML FORM and submit button. We use same CGI script hello_get.py to handle this input.

```
<form action = "/cgi-bin/hello_get.py" method = "get">

First Name: <input type = "text" name = "first_name">
<br />


Last Name: <input type = "text" name = "last_name" />

<input type = "submit" value = "Submit" />

</form>
```

Here is the actual output of the above form, you enter First and Last Name and then click submit button to see the result.

FirstName:

Last Name:

Submit

Passing Information Using POST Method

A generally more reliable method of passing information to a CGI program is the POST method. This packages the information in exactly the same way as GET methods, but instead of sending it as a text string after a ? in the URL it sends it as a separate message. This message comes into the CGI script in the form of the standard input.

Below is same hello_get.py script which handles GET as well as POST method.

```
#!/usr/bin/python


# Import modules for CGI handling

import cgi, cgitb


# Create instance of FieldStorage

form = cgi.FieldStorage()
```

```python
# Get data from fields

first_name = form.getvalue('first_name')

last_name = form.getvalue('last_name')


print "Content-type:text/html\r\n\r\n"

print "<html>"

print "<head>"

print "<title>Hello - Second CGI Program</title>"

print "</head>"

print "<body>"

print "<h2>Hello %s %s</h2>" % (first_name, last_name)

print "</body>"

print "</html>"
```

Let us take again same example as above which passes two values using HTML FORM and submit button. We use same CGI script hello_get.py to handle this input.

```html
<form action = "/cgi-bin/hello_get.py" method = "post">

First Name: <input type = "text" name = "first_name"><br
/>
```

```
Last Name: <input type = "text" name = "last_name" />

<input type = "submit" value = "Submit" />
</form>
```

Here is the actual output of the above form. You enter First and Last Name and then click submit button to see the result:

First Name: ☐
Last Name: ☐

Submit

Passing Checkbox Data to CGI Program:

Checkboxes are used when more than one option is required to be selected.

Here is example HTML code for a form with two checkboxes –

```
<form action = "/cgi-bin/checkbox.cgi" method = "POST"
target = "_blank">
```

```
<input type = "checkbox" name = "maths" value = "on" />
Maths

<input type = "checkbox" name = "physics" value = "on" />
Physics

<input type = "submit" value = "Select Subject" />

</form>
```

The result of this code is the following form –

⌐ **Maths** ⌐ **Physics**

[Select Subject]

Below is checkbox.cgi script to handle input given by web browser for checkbox button.

```python
#!/usr/bin/python


# Import modules for CGI handling

import cgi, cgitb


# Create instance of FieldStorage

form = cgi.FieldStorage()
```

```python
# Get data from fields
if form.getvalue('maths'):
  math_flag = "ON"
else:
  math_flag = "OFF"


if form.getvalue('physics'):
  physics_flag = "ON"
else:
  physics_flag = "OFF"


print "Content-type:text/html\r\n\r\n"
print "<html>"
print "<head>"
print "<title>Checkbox - Third CGI Program</title>"
print "</head>"
print "<body>"
print "<h2> CheckBox Maths is : %s</h2>" % math_flag
```

```
print "<h2> CheckBox Physics is : %s</h2>" %
physics_flag

print "</body>"

print "</html>"
```

Passing Radio Button Data to CGI Program:

Radio Buttons are used when only one option is required to be selected.

Here is example HTML code for a form with two radio buttons −

```
<form action = "/cgi-bin/radiobutton.py" method = "post"
target = "_blank">

<input type = "radio" name = "subject" value = "maths" />
Maths

<input type = "radio" name = "subject" value = "physics"
/> Physics

<input type = "submit" value = "Select Subject" />

</form>
```

The result of this code is the following form −

C **Maths** C **Physics**

Select Subject

Below is radiobutton.py script to handle input given by web browser for radio button −

```
#!/usr/bin/python


# Import modules for CGI handling
import cgi, cgitb


# Create instance of FieldStorage
form = cgi.FieldStorage()


# Get data from fields
if form.getvalue('subject'):
    subject = form.getvalue('subject')
else:
    subject = "Not set"
```

```
print "Content-type:text/html\r\n\r\n"

print "<html>"

print "<head>"

print "<title>Radio - Fourth CGI Program</title>"

print "</head>"

print "<body>"

print "<h2> Selected Subject is %s</h2>" % subject

print "</body>"

print "</html>"
```

Passing Text Area Data to CGI Program:

TEXTAREA element is used when multiline text has to be passed to the CGI Program.

Here is example HTML code for a form with a TEXTAREA box –

```
<form action = "/cgi-bin/textarea.py" method = "post"
target = "_blank">

<textarea name = "textcontent" cols = "40" rows = "4">

Type your text here...

</textarea>
```

```
<input type = "submit" value = "Submit" />

</form>
```

The result of this code is the following form –

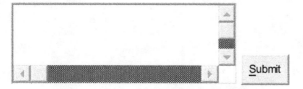

Below is textarea.cgi script to handle input given by web browser –

```
#!/usr/bin/python


# Import modules for CGI handling

import cgi, cgitb


# Create instance of FieldStorage

form = cgi.FieldStorage()


# Get data from fields

if form.getvalue('textcontent'):

    text_content = form.getvalue('textcontent')
```

```
else:

  text_content = "Not entered"


print "Content-type:text/html\r\n\r\n"

print "<html>"

print "<head>";

print "<title>Text Area - Fifth CGI Program</title>"

print "</head>"

print "<body>"

print "<h2> Entered Text Content is %s</h2>" %
text_content

print "</body>"
```

Passing Drop Down Box Data to CGI Program

Drop Down Box is used when we have many options available but only one or two will be selected.

Here is example HTML code for a form with one drop down box −

```
<form action = "/cgi-bin/dropdown.py" method = "post"
target = "_blank">

<select name = "dropdown">
```

```
<option value = "Maths" selected>Maths</option>

<option value = "Physics">Physics</option>

</select>

<input type = "submit" value = "Submit"/>

</form>
```

The result of this code is the following form –

Below is dropdown.py script to handle input given by web browser.

```
#!/usr/bin/python


# Import modules for CGI handling

import cgi, cgitb


# Create instance of FieldStorage

form = cgi.FieldStorage()


# Get data from fields
```

```
if form.getvalue('dropdown'):

  subject = form.getvalue('dropdown')

else:

  subject = "Not entered"


print "Content-type:text/html\r\n\r\n"

print "<html>"

print "<head>"

print "<title>Dropdown Box - Sixth CGI Program</title>"

print "</head>"

print "<body>"

print "<h2> Selected Subject is %s</h2>" % subject

print "</body>"

print "</html>"
```

Using Cookies in CGI:

HTTP protocol is a stateless protocol. For a commercial website, it is required to maintain session information among different pages. For example, one user registration ends after completing many pages. How to maintain user's session information across all the web pages?

In many situations, using cookies is the most efficient method of remembering and tracking preferences, purchases, commissions, and other information required for better visitor experience or site statistics.

How It Works?

Your server sends some data to the visitor's browser in the form of a cookie. The browser may accept the cookie. If it does, it is stored as a plain text record on the visitor's hard drive. Now, when the visitor arrives at another page on your site, the cookie is available for retrieval. Once retrieved, your server knows/remembers what was stored.

Cookies are a plain text data record of 5 variable-length fields –

- **Expires** – The date the cookie will expire. If this is blank, the cookie will expire when the visitor quits the browser.

- **Domain** – The domain name of your site.

- **Path** – The path to the directory or web page that sets the cookie. This may be blank if you want to retrieve the cookie from any directory or page.

- **Secure** – If this field contains the word "secure", then the cookie may only be retrieved with a secure server. If this field is blank, no such restriction exists.

- **Name=Value** – Cookies are set and retrieved in the form of key and value pairs.

Setting up Cookies

It is very easy to send cookies to browser. These cookies are sent along with HTTP Header before to Content-type field. Assuming you want to set UserID and Password as cookies. Setting the cookies is done as follows –

```
#!/usr/bin/python


print "Set-Cookie:UserID = XYZ;\r\n"

print "Set-Cookie:Password = XYZ123;\r\n"

print "Set-Cookie:Expires = Tuesday, 31-Dec-2007 23:12:40 GMT";\r\n"

print "Set-Cookie:Domain = www.google.com;\r\n"

print "Set-Cookie:Path = /perl;\n"

print "Content-type:text/html\r\n\r\n"

..........Rest of the HTML Content....
```

From this example, you must have understood how to set cookies. We use **Set-Cookie** HTTP header to set cookies.

It is optional to set cookies attributes like Expires, Domain, and Path. It is notable that cookies are set before sending magic line **"Content-type:text/html\r\n\r\n.**

Retrieving Cookies

It is very easy to retrieve all the set cookies. Cookies are stored in CGI environment variable HTTP_COOKIE and they will have following form –

```
key1 = value1;key2 = value2;key3 = value3....
```

Here is an example of how to retrieve cookies.

```
#!/usr/bin/python


# Import modules for CGI handling

from os import environ

import cgi, cgitb


if environ.has_key('HTTP_COOKIE'):

   for cookie in map(strip, split(environ['HTTP_COOKIE'],
';')):
```

```
(key, value ) = split(cookie, '=');

if key == "UserID":

    user_id = value


if key == "Password":

    password = value


print "User ID  = %s" % user_id

print "Password = %s" % password
```

This produces the following result for the cookies set by above script –

```
User ID = XYZ
Password = XYZ123
```

File Upload Example:

To upload a file, the HTML form must have the enctype attribute set to **multipart/form-data**. The input tag with the file type creates a "Browse" button.

```
<html>

<body>
```

```
<form enctype = "multipart/form-data"
          action = "save_file.py" method = "post">
<p>File: <input type = "file" name = "filename" /></p>
<p><input type = "submit" value = "Upload" /></p>
</form>
</body>
</html>
```

The result of this code is the following form −

File:

Upload

Above example has been disabled intentionally to save people uploading file on our server, but you can try above code with your server.

Here is the script **save_file.py** to handle file upload −

```
#!/usr/bin/python


import cgi, os
import cgitb; cgitb.enable()
```

```python
form = cgi.FieldStorage()


# Get filename here.

fileitem = form['filename']


# Test if the file was uploaded

if fileitem.filename:

    # strip leading path from file name to avoid

    # directory traversal attacks

    fn = os.path.basename(fileitem.filename)

    open('/tmp/' + fn, 'wb').write(fileitem.file.read())


    message = 'The file "' + fn + '" was uploaded successfully'


else:

    message = 'No file was uploaded'


print """\
Content-Type: text/html\n
```

```
<html>
<body>
  <p>%s</p>
</body>
</html>
""" % (message,)
```

If you run the above script on Unix/Linux, then you need to take care of replacing file separator as follows, otherwise on your windows machine above open() statement should work fine.

```
fn = os.path.basename(fileitem.filename.replace("\\", "/" ))
```

How To Raise a "File Download" Dialog Box?

Sometimes, it is desired that you want to give option where a user can click a link and it will pop up a "File Download" dialogue box to the user instead of displaying actual content. This is very easy and can be achieved through HTTP header. This HTTP header is be different from the header mentioned in previous section.

For example, if you want make a **FileName** file downloadable from a given link, then its syntax is as follows –

```
#!/usr/bin/python
```

```python
# HTTP Header

print "Content-Type:application/octet-stream; name =
\"FileName\"\r\n";

print "Content-Disposition: attachment; filename =
\"FileName\"\r\n\n";


# Actual File Content will go here.

fo = open("foo.txt", "rb")


str = fo.read();

print str


# Close opend file

fo.close()
```

Python - MySQL Database Access

The Python standard for database interfaces is the Python DB-API. Most Python database interfaces adhere to this standard.

You can choose the right database for your application. Python Database API supports a wide range of database servers such as –

- GadFly
- mSQL
- MySQL
- PostgreSQL
- Microsoft SQL Server 2000
- Informix
- Interbase
- Oracle
- Sybase

Here is the list of available Python database interfaces: Python Database Interfaces and APIs. You must download a separate DB API module for each database you need to access. For example, if you need to access an Oracle database as well as a MySQL database, you must download both the Oracle and the MySQL database modules.

The DB API provides a minimal standard for working with databases using Python structures and syntax wherever possible. This API includes the following –

- Importing the API module.
- Acquiring a connection with the database.
- Issuing SQL statements and stored procedures.
- Closing the connection

We would learn all the concepts using MySQL, so let us talk about MySQLdb module.

What is MySQLdb?

MySQLdb is an interface for connecting to a MySQL database server from Python. It implements the Python Database API v2.0 and is built on top of the MySQL C API.

How do I Install MySQLdb?

Before proceeding, you make sure you have MySQLdb installed on your machine. Just type the following in your Python script and execute it –

```
#!/usr/bin/python
```

```
import MySQLdb
```

If it produces the following result, then it means MySQLdb module is not installed –

```
Traceback (most recent call last):
  File "test.py", line 3, in <module>
    import MySQLdb
ImportError: No module named MySQLdb
```

To install MySQLdb module, use the following command –

```
For Ubuntu, use the following command -
$   sudo   apt-get   install   python-pip   python-dev
libmysqlclient-dev
For Fedora, use the following command -
$ sudo dnf install python python-devel mysql-devel redhat-
rpm-config gcc
For Python command prompt, use the following command
-
pip install MySQL-python
```

Note – Make sure you have root privilege to install above module.

Database Connection

Before connecting to a MySQL database, make sure of the followings –

- You have created a database TESTDB.

- You have created a table EMPLOYEE in TESTDB.

- This table has fields FIRST_NAME, LAST_NAME, AGE, SEX and INCOME.

- User ID "testuser" and password "test123" are set to access TESTDB.

- Python module MySQLdb is installed properly on your machine.

- You have gone through MySQL tutorial to understand MySQL Basics.

Example

Following is the example of connecting with MySQL database "TESTDB"

```
#!/usr/bin/python


import MySQLdb


# Open database connection

db                                          =
MySQLdb.connect("localhost","testuser","test123","TEST
DB" )
```

```
# prepare a cursor object using cursor() method

cursor = db.cursor()


# execute SQL query using execute() method.

cursor.execute("SELECT VERSION()")


# Fetch a single row using fetchone() method.

data = cursor.fetchone()

print "Database version : %s " % data


# disconnect from server

db.close()
```

While running this script, it is producing the following result in my Linux machine.

Database version : 5.0.45

If a connection is established with the datasource, then a Connection Object is returned and saved into **db** for further use, otherwise **db** is set to None. Next, **db** object is used to create a **cursor** object, which in turn is used to execute SQL queries. Finally, before coming out, it ensures that database connection is closed and resources are released.

Creating Database Table:

Once a database connection is established, we are ready to create tables or records into the database tables using **execute** method of the created cursor.

Example

Let us create Database table EMPLOYEE –

```
#!/usr/bin/python


import MySQLdb


# Open database connection
db                                           =
MySQLdb.connect("localhost","testuser","test123","TEST
DB" )


# prepare a cursor object using cursor() method
cursor = db.cursor()


# Drop table if it already exist using execute() method.
```

```
cursor.execute("DROP TABLE IF EXISTS EMPLOYEE")


# Create table as per requirement
sql = """CREATE TABLE EMPLOYEE (

    FIRST_NAME  CHAR(20) NOT NULL,

    LAST_NAME  CHAR(20),

    AGE INT,

    SEX CHAR(1),

    INCOME FLOAT )"""


cursor.execute(sql)


# disconnect from server
db.close()
```

INSERT Operation:

It is required when you want to create your records into a database table.

Example

The following example, executes SQL *INSERT* statement to create a record into EMPLOYEE table −

```
#!/usr/bin/python


import MySQLdb


# Open database connection
db = MySQLdb.connect("localhost","testuser","test123","TEST DB" )


# prepare a cursor object using cursor() method
cursor = db.cursor()


# Prepare SQL query to INSERT a record into the database.
sql = """INSERT INTO EMPLOYEE(FIRST_NAME,
    LAST_NAME, AGE, SEX, INCOME)
    VALUES ('Mac', 'Mohan', 20, 'M', 2000)"""
try:
```

```
    # Execute the SQL command

    cursor.execute(sql)

    # Commit your changes in the database

    db.commit()

except:

    # Rollback in case there is any error

    db.rollback()


# disconnect from server

db.close()
```

Above example can be written as follows to create SQL queries dynamically −

```
#!/usr/bin/python


import MySQLdb


# Open database connection
db                                        =
MySQLdb.connect("localhost","testuser","test123","TEST
DB" )
```

```
# prepare a cursor object using cursor() method
cursor = db.cursor()


# Prepare SQL query to INSERT a record into the database.
sql = "INSERT INTO EMPLOYEE(FIRST_NAME, \
    LAST_NAME, AGE, SEX, INCOME) \
    VALUES ('%s', '%s', '%d', '%c', '%d' )" % \
    ('Mac', 'Mohan', 20, 'M', 2000)
try:
  # Execute the SQL command
  cursor.execute(sql)
  # Commit your changes in the database
  db.commit()
except:
  # Rollback in case there is any error
  db.rollback()


# disconnect from server
```

```
db.close()
```

Example

Following code segment is another form of execution where you can pass parameters directly –

```
........................................
user_id = "test123"
password = "password"

con.execute('insert into Login values("%s", "%s")' % \
        (user_id, password))
........................................
```

READ Operation:

READ Operation on any database means to fetch some useful information from the database.

Once our database connection is established, you are ready to make a query into this database. You can use either **fetchone()**method to fetch single record or **fetchall()** method to fetech multiple values from a database table.

- **fetchone()** – It fetches the next row of a query result set. A result set is an object that is returned when a cursor object is used to query a table.

- **fetchall()** – It fetches all the rows in a result set. If some rows have already been extracted from the result set, then it retrieves the remaining rows from the result set.

- **rowcount** – This is a read-only attribute and returns the number of rows that were affected by an execute() method.

Example

The following procedure queries all the records from EMPLOYEE table having salary more than 1000 –

```
#!/usr/bin/python


import MySQLdb


# Open database connection

db                                                    =
MySQLdb.connect("localhost","testuser","test123","TEST
DB" )


# prepare a cursor object using cursor() method

cursor = db.cursor()
```

```python
sql = "SELECT * FROM EMPLOYEE \
       WHERE INCOME > '%d'" % (1000)
try:
   # Execute the SQL command
   cursor.execute(sql)
   # Fetch all the rows in a list of lists.
   results = cursor.fetchall()
   for row in results:
      fname = row[0]
      lname = row[1]
      age = row[2]
      sex = row[3]
      income = row[4]
      # Now print fetched result
      print "fname=%s,lname=%s,age=%d,sex=%s,income=%d" % \
            (fname, lname, age, sex, income )
except:
   print "Error: unable to fecth data"
```

```
# disconnect from server

db.close()
```

This will produce the following result –

```
fname=Mac, lname=Mohan, age=20, sex=M, income=2000
```

Update Operation:

UPDATE Operation on any database means to update one or more records, which are already available in the database.

The following procedure updates all the records having SEX as **'M'**. Here, we increase AGE of all the males by one year.

Example

```
#!/usr/bin/python


import MySQLdb


# Open database connection

db                                    =
MySQLdb.connect("localhost","testuser","test123","TEST
DB" )
```

```python
# prepare a cursor object using cursor() method

cursor = db.cursor()


# Prepare SQL query to UPDATE required records

sql = "UPDATE EMPLOYEE SET AGE = AGE + 1
                WHERE SEX = '%c'" % ('M')
try:
   # Execute the SQL command

   cursor.execute(sql)

   # Commit your changes in the database

   db.commit()
except:
   # Rollback in case there is any error

   db.rollback()


# disconnect from server

db.close()
```

DELETE Operation:

DELETE operation is required when you want to delete some records from your database. Following is the procedure to delete all the records from EMPLOYEE where AGE is more than 20 –

Example

```
#!/usr/bin/python

import MySQLdb

# Open database connection
db                                           =
MySQLdb.connect("localhost","testuser","test123","TEST
DB" )

# prepare a cursor object using cursor() method
cursor = db.cursor()

# Prepare SQL query to DELETE required records
```

```
sql = "DELETE FROM EMPLOYEE WHERE AGE >
'%d'" % (20)

try:

   # Execute the SQL command

   cursor.execute(sql)

   # Commit your changes in the database

   db.commit()

except:

   # Rollback in case there is any error

   db.rollback()


# disconnect from server

db.close()
```

Performing Transactions:

Transactions are a mechanism that ensures data consistency. Transactions have the following four properties –

- **Atomicity** – Either a transaction completes or nothing happens at all.

- **Consistency** – A transaction must start in a consistent state and leave the system in a consistent state.

- **Isolation** – Intermediate results of a transaction are not visible outside the current transaction.

- **Durability** – Once a transaction was committed, the effects are persistent, even after a system failure.

The Python DB API 2.0 provides two methods to either *commit* or *rollback* a transaction.

Example

You already know how to implement transactions. Here is again similar example –

```
# Prepare SQL query to DELETE required records

sql = "DELETE FROM EMPLOYEE WHERE AGE > '%d'" % (20)

try:

  # Execute the SQL command

  cursor.execute(sql)

  # Commit your changes in the database

  db.commit()
```

```
except:

    # Rollback in case there is any error

    db.rollback()
```

COMMIT Operation:

Commit is the operation, which gives a green signal to database to finalize the changes, and after this operation, no change can be reverted back.

Here is a simple example to call **commit** method.

```
db.commit()
```

ROLLBACK Operation:

If you are not satisfied with one or more of the changes and you want to revert back those changes completely, then use **rollback()** method.

Here is a simple example to call **rollback()** method.

```
db.rollback()
```

Disconnecting Database:

To disconnect Database connection, use close() method.

```
db.close()
```

If the connection to a database is closed by the user with the close() method, any outstanding transactions are rolled back by the DB. However, instead of depending on any of DB lower level implementation details, your application would be better off calling commit or rollback explicitly.

Handling Errors:

There are many sources of errors. A few examples are a syntax error in an executed SQL statement, a connection failure, or calling the fetch method for an already canceled or finished statement handle.

The DB API defines a number of errors that must exist in each database module. The following table lists these exceptions.

Sr.No.	Exception & Description
1	**Warning** Used for non-fatal issues. Must subclass StandardError.
2	**Error** Base class for errors. Must subclass StandardError.

3	**InterfaceError**
	Used for errors in the database module, not the database itself. Must subclass Error.
4	**DatabaseError**
	Used for errors in the database. Must subclass Error.
5	**DataError**
	Subclass of DatabaseError that refers to errors in the data.
6	**OperationalError**
	Subclass of DatabaseError that refers to errors such as the loss of a connection to the database. These errors are generally outside of the control of the Python scripter.
7	**IntegrityError**
	Subclass of DatabaseError for situations that would damage the relational integrity, such as uniqueness constraints or foreign keys.

8	**InternalError**
	Subclass of DatabaseError that refers to errors internal to the database module, such as a cursor no longer being active.
9	**ProgrammingError**
	Subclass of DatabaseError that refers to errors such as a bad table name and other things that can safely be blamed on you.
10	**NotSupportedError**
	Subclass of DatabaseError that refers to trying to call unsupported functionality.

Your Python scripts should handle these errors, but before using any of the above exceptions, make sure your MySQLdb has support for that exception. You can get more information about them by reading the DB API 2.0 specification.

Python - Network Programming

Python provides two levels of access to network services. At a low level, you can access the basic socket support in the underlying operating system, which allows you to implement clients and servers for both connection-oriented and connectionless protocols.

Python also has libraries that provide higher-level access to specific application-level network protocols, such as FTP, HTTP, and so on.

This chapter gives you understanding on most famous concept in Networking - Socket Programming.

What is Sockets?

Sockets are the endpoints of a bidirectional communications channel. Sockets may communicate within a process, between processes on the same machine, or between processes on different continents.

Sockets may be implemented over a number of different channel types: Unix domain sockets, TCP, UDP, and so on. The *socket* library provides specific classes for handling the common transports as well as a generic interface for handling the rest.

Sockets have their own vocabulary –

Sr.No.	Term & Description
1	**Domain** The family of protocols that is used as the transport mechanism. These values are constants such as AF_INET, PF_INET, PF_UNIX, PF_X25, and so on.
2	**type** The type of communications between the two endpoints, typically SOCK_STREAM for connection-oriented protocols and SOCK_DGRAM for connectionless protocols.
3	**protocol** Typically zero, this may be used to identify a variant of a protocol within a domain and type.
4	**hostname** The identifier of a network interface – • A string, which can be a host name, a dotted-quad address, or an IPV6 address in colon (and possibly dot) notation

	• A string "<broadcast>", which specifies an INADDR_BROADCAST address. • A zero-length string, which specifies INADDR_ANY, or • An Integer, interpreted as a binary address in host byte order.
5	**port** Each server listens for clients calling on one or more ports. A port may be a Fixnum port number, a string containing a port number, or the name of a service.

The *socket* Module:

To create a socket, you must use the *socket.socket()* function available in *socket* module, which has the general syntax −

```
s = socket.socket (socket_family, socket_type, protocol=0)
```

Here is the description of the parameters −

• **socket_family** − This is either AF_UNIX or AF_INET, as explained earlier.

- **socket_type** – This is either SOCK_STREAM or SOCK_DGRAM.

- **protocol** – This is usually left out, defaulting to 0.

Once you have *socket* object, then you can use required functions to create your client or server program. Following is the list of functions required –

Server Socket Methods:

Sr.No.	Method & Description
1	**s.bind()** This method binds address (hostname, port number pair) to socket.
2	**s.listen()** This method sets up and start TCP listener.
3	**s.accept()** This passively accept TCP client connection, waiting until connection arrives (blocking).

Client Socket Methods

Sr.No.	Method & Description
1	**s.connect()** This method actively initiates TCP server connection.

General Socket Methods

Sr.No.	Method & Description
1	**s.recv()** This method receives TCP message
2	**s.send()** This method transmits TCP message
3	**s.recvfrom()** This method receives UDP message
4	**s.sendto()** This method transmits UDP message

5	**s.close()**
	This method closes socket
6	**socket.gethostname()**
	Returns the hostname.

A Simple Server:

To write Internet servers, we use the **socket** function available in socket module to create a socket object. A socket object is then used to call other functions to setup a socket server.

Now call **bind(hostname, port)** function to specify a *port* for your service on the given host.

Next, call the *accept* method of the returned object. This method waits until a client connects to the port you specified, and then returns a *connection* object that represents the connection to that client.

```
#!/usr/bin/python        # This is server.py file


import socket        # Import socket module
```

```
s = socket.socket()      # Create a socket object

host = socket.gethostname() # Get local machine name

port = 12345             # Reserve a port for your service.

s.bind((host, port))     # Bind to the port


s.listen(5)              # Now wait for client connection.

while True:

  c, addr = s.accept()   # Establish connection with client.

  print 'Got connection from', addr

  c.send('Thank you for connecting')

  c.close()              # Close the connection
```

A Simple Client

Let us write a very simple client program which opens a connection to a given port 12345 and given host. This is very simple to create a socket client using Python's *socket* module function.

The **socket.connect(hosname, port)** opens a TCP connection to *hostname* on the *port*. Once you have a socket open, you can read from it like any IO object.

When done, remember to close it, as you would close a file.

The following code is a very simple client that connects to a given host and port, reads any available data from the socket, and then exits −

```python
#!/usr/bin/python         # This is client.py file


import socket              # Import socket module


s = socket.socket()       # Create a socket object
host = socket.gethostname() # Get local machine name
port = 12345              # Reserve a port for your service.


s.connect((host, port))
print s.recv(1024)
s.close()                 # Close the socket when done
```

Now run this server.py in background and then run above client.py to see the result.

```
# Following would start a server in background.
$ python server.py &
```

```
# Once server is started run client as follows:

$ python client.py
```

This would produce following result –

```
Got connection from ('127.0.0.1', 48437)
Thank you for connecting
```

Python Internet modules

A list of some important modules in Python Network/Internet programming.

Protocol	Common function	Port No	Python module
HTTP	Web pages	80	httplib, urllib, xmlrpclib
NNTP	Usenet news	119	nntplib
FTP	File transfers	20	ftplib, urllib
SMTP	Sending email	25	smtplib

POP3	Fetching email	110	poplib
IMAP4	Fetching email	143	imaplib
Telnet	Command lines	23	telnetlib
Gopher	Document transfers	70	gopherlib, urllib

Please check all the libraries mentioned above to work with FTP, SMTP, POP, and IMAP protocols.

Python - Sending Email using SMTP

Simple Mail Transfer Protocol (SMTP) is a protocol, which handles sending e-mail and routing e-mail between mail servers.

Python provides **smtplib** module, which defines an SMTP client session object that can be used to send mail to any Internet machine with an SMTP or ESMTP listener daemon.

Here is a simple syntax to create one SMTP object, which can later be used to send an e-mail −

```
import smtplib


smtpObj   =   smtplib.SMTP(   [host   [,   port   [,
local_hostname]]] )
```

Here is the detail of the parameters −

- **host** − This is the host running your SMTP server. You can specify IP address of the host or a domain name like google.com. This is optional argument.

- **port** − If you are providing *host* argument, then you need to specify a port, where SMTP server is listening. Usually this port would be 25.

- **local_hostname** − If your SMTP server is running on your local machine, then you can specify just *localhost* as of this option.

An SMTP object has an instance method called **sendmail**, which is typically used to do the work of mailing a message. It takes three parameters –

- The *sender* – A string with the address of the sender.

- The *receivers* – A list of strings, one for each recipient.

- The *message* – A message as a string formatted as specified in the various RFCs.

Example

Here is a simple way to send one e-mail using Python script. Try it once –

```
#!/usr/bin/python


import smtplib


sender = 'from@fromdomain.com'

receivers = ['to@todomain.com']


message = """From: From Person
<from@fromdomain.com>
```

```
To: To Person <to@todomain.com>

Subject: SMTP e-mail test


This is a test e-mail message.
"""


try:

    smtpObj = smtplib.SMTP('localhost')

    smtpObj.sendmail(sender, receivers, message)

    print "Successfully sent email"

except SMTPException:

    print "Error: unable to send email"
```

Here, you have placed a basic e-mail in message, using a triple quote, taking care to format the headers correctly. An e-mail requires a **From, To,** and **Subject** header, separated from the body of the e-mail with a blank line.

To send the mail you use *smtpObj* to connect to the SMTP server on the local machine and then use the *sendmail* method along with the message, the from address, and the destination address as parameters (even though the from and to addresses are within the e-mail itself, these aren't always used to route mail).

If you are not running an SMTP server on your local machine, you can use *smtplib* client to communicate with a remote SMTP server. Unless you are using a webmail service (such as Hotmail or Yahoo! Mail), your e-mail provider must have provided you with outgoing mail server details that you can supply them, as follows –

```
smtplib.SMTP('mail.your-domain.com', 25)
```

Sending an HTML e-mail using Python:

When you send a text message using Python, then all the content are treated as simple text. Even if you include HTML tags in a text message, it is displayed as simple text and HTML tags will not be formatted according to HTML syntax. But Python provides option to send an HTML message as actual HTML message.

While sending an e-mail message, you can specify a Mime version, content type and character set to send an HTML e-mail.

Example:

Following is the example to send HTML content as an e-mail. Try it once –

```
#!/usr/bin/python

import smtplib

message = """From: From Person <from@fromdomain.com>
To: To Person <to@todomain.com>
MIME-Version: 1.0
Content-type: text/html
Subject: SMTP HTML e-mail test

This is an e-mail message to be sent in HTML format

<b>This is HTML message.</b>
<h1>This is headline.</h1>
"""

try:
   smtpObj = smtplib.SMTP('localhost')
   smtpObj.sendmail(sender, receivers, message)
```

```
   print "Successfully sent email"

except SMTPException:

   print "Error: unable to send email"
```

Sending Attachments as an E-mail:

To send an e-mail with mixed content requires to set **Content-type** header to **multipart/mixed**. Then, text and attachment sections can be specified within **boundaries**.

A boundary is started with two hyphens followed by a unique number, which cannot appear in the message part of the e-mail. A final boundary denoting the e-mail's final section must also end with two hyphens.

Attached files should be encoded with the **pack("m")** function to have base64 encoding before transmission.

Example:

Following is the example, which sends a file **/tmp/test.txt** as an attachment. Try it once –

```
#!/usr/bin/python


import smtplib
```

```
import base64

filename = "/tmp/test.txt"


# Read a file and encode it into base64 format
fo = open(filename, "rb")
filecontent = fo.read()
encodedcontent = base64.b64encode(filecontent)  # base64


sender = 'webmaster@tutorialpoint.com'
reciever = 'amrood.admin@gmail.com'


marker = "AUNIQUEMARKER"


body ="""
This is a test email to send an attachement.
"""

# Define the main headers.
part1 = """From: From Person <me@fromdomain.net>
```

```
To: To Person <amrood.admin@gmail.com>

Subject: Sending Attachement

MIME-Version: 1.0

Content-Type: multipart/mixed; boundary=%s

--%s

""" % (marker, marker)


# Define the message action

part2 = """Content-Type: text/plain

Content-Transfer-Encoding:8bit


%s
--%s

""" % (body,marker)


# Define the attachment section

part3 = """Content-Type: multipart/mixed; name=\"%s\"

Content-Transfer-Encoding:base64

Content-Disposition: attachment; filename=%s
```

```
%s

--%s--

""" %(filename, filename, encodedcontent, marker)

message = part1 + part2 + part3


try:

    smtpObj = smtplib.SMTP('localhost')

    smtpObj.sendmail(sender, reciever, message)

    print "Successfully sent email"

except Exception:

    print "Error: unable to send email"
```

Python - Multithreaded Programming

Running several threads is similar to running several different programs concurrently, but with the following benefits –

- Multiple threads within a process share the same data space with the main thread and can therefore share information or communicate with each other more easily than if they were separate processes.

- Threads sometimes called light-weight processes and they do not require much memory overhead; they are cheaper than processes.

A thread has a beginning, an execution sequence, and a conclusion. It has an instruction pointer that keeps track of where within its context it is currently running.

- It can be pre-empted (interrupted)

- It can temporarily be put on hold (also known as sleeping) while other threads are running - this is called yielding.

Starting a New Thread:

To spawn another thread, you need to call following method available in *thread* module –

```
thread.start_new_thread ( function, args[, kwargs] )
```

This method call enables a fast and efficient way to create new threads in both Linux and Windows.

The method call returns immediately and the child thread starts and calls function with the passed list of *args*. When function returns, the thread terminates.

Here, *args* is a tuple of arguments; use an empty tuple to call function without passing any arguments. *kwargs* is an optional dictionary of keyword arguments.

Example

```python
#!/usr/bin/python


import thread

import time


# Define a function for the thread
def print_time( threadName, delay):

    count = 0

    while count < 5:

        time.sleep(delay)

        count += 1
```

```
    print     "%s:     %s"     %     (     threadName,
time.ctime(time.time()) )


# Create two threads as follows

try:

    thread.start_new_thread( print_time, ("Thread-1", 2, ) )

    thread.start_new_thread( print_time, ("Thread-2", 4, ) )

except:

    print "Error: unable to start thread"


while 1:

    pass
```

When the above code is executed, it produces the following result –

```
Thread-1: Thu Jan 22 15:42:17 2009
Thread-1: Thu Jan 22 15:42:19 2009
Thread-2: Thu Jan 22 15:42:19 2009
Thread-1: Thu Jan 22 15:42:21 2009
Thread-2: Thu Jan 22 15:42:23 2009
Thread-1: Thu Jan 22 15:42:23 2009
Thread-1: Thu Jan 22 15:42:25 2009
Thread-2: Thu Jan 22 15:42:27 2009
Thread-2: Thu Jan 22 15:42:31 2009
Thread-2: Thu Jan 22 15:42:35 2009
```

Although it is very effective for low-level threading, but the *thread* module is very limited compared to the newer threading module.

The *Threading* Module:

The newer threading module included with Python 2.4 provides much more powerful, high-level support for threads than the thread module discussed in the previous section.

The *threading* module exposes all the methods of the *thread* module and provides some additional methods −

- **threading.activeCount()** − Returns the number of thread objects that are active.

- **threading.currentThread()** − Returns the number of thread objects in the caller's thread control.

- **threading.enumerate()** − Returns a list of all thread objects that are currently active.

In addition to the methods, the threading module has the *Thread* class that implements threading. The methods provided by the *Thread* class are as follows −

- **run()** − The run() method is the entry point for a thread.

- **start()** − The start() method starts a thread by calling the run method.

- **join([time])** – The join() waits for threads to terminate.

- **isAlive()** – The isAlive() method checks whether a thread is still executing.

- **getName()** – The getName() method returns the name of a thread.

- **setName()** – The setName() method sets the name of a thread.

Creating Thread Using *Threading* Module:

To implement a new thread using the threading module, you have to do the following –

- Define a new subclass of the *Thread* class.

- Override the __init__(self [,args]) method to add additional arguments.

- Then, override the run(self [,args]) method to implement what the thread should do when started.

Once you have created the new *Thread* subclass, you can create an instance of it and then start a new thread by invoking the *start()*, which in turn calls *run()* method.

Example

```python
#!/usr/bin/python


import threading
import time


exitFlag = 0


class myThread (threading.Thread):
  def __init__(self, threadID, name, counter):
    threading.Thread.__init__(self)
    self.threadID = threadID
    self.name = name
    self.counter = counter
  def run(self):
    print "Starting " + self.name
    print_time(self.name, self.counter, 5)
    print "Exiting " + self.name
```

```python
def print_time(threadName, counter, delay):

    while counter:

        if exitFlag:

            threadName.exit()

        time.sleep(delay)

        print      "%s:      %s"      %      (threadName,
time.ctime(time.time()))

        counter -= 1


# Create new threads

thread1 = myThread(1, "Thread-1", 1)

thread2 = myThread(2, "Thread-2", 2)


# Start new Threads

thread1.start()

thread2.start()


print "Exiting Main Thread"
```

When the above code is executed, it produces the following result −

```
Starting Thread-1
Starting Thread-2
Exiting Main Thread
Thread-1: Thu Mar 21 09:10:03 2013
Thread-1: Thu Mar 21 09:10:04 2013
Thread-2: Thu Mar 21 09:10:04 2013
Thread-1: Thu Mar 21 09:10:05 2013
Thread-1: Thu Mar 21 09:10:06 2013
Thread-2: Thu Mar 21 09:10:06 2013
Thread-1: Thu Mar 21 09:10:07 2013
Exiting Thread-1
Thread-2: Thu Mar 21 09:10:08 2013
Thread-2: Thu Mar 21 09:10:10 2013
Thread-2: Thu Mar 21 09:10:12 2013
Exiting Thread-2
```

Synchronizing Threads:

The threading module provided with Python includes a simple-to-implement locking mechanism that allows you to synchronize threads. A new lock is created by calling the *Lock()* method, which returns the new lock.

The *acquire(blocking)* method of the new lock object is used to force threads to run synchronously. The optional *blocking*parameter enables you to control whether the thread waits to acquire the lock.

If *blocking* is set to 0, the thread returns immediately with a 0 value if the lock cannot be acquired and with a 1 if the lock was acquired. If blocking is set to 1, the thread blocks and wait for the lock to be released.

The *release()* method of the new lock object is used to release the lock when it is no longer required.

Example:

```python
#!/usr/bin/python


import threading

import time


class myThread (threading.Thread):
    def __init__(self, threadID, name, counter):
        threading.Thread.__init__(self)
        self.threadID = threadID
        self.name = name
        self.counter = counter
    def run(self):
        print "Starting " + self.name
```

```
        # Get lock to synchronize threads

        threadLock.acquire()

        print_time(self.name, self.counter, 3)

        # Free lock to release next thread

        threadLock.release()


def print_time(threadName, delay, counter):

  while counter:

    time.sleep(delay)

    print      "%s:      %s"      %      (threadName,
time.ctime(time.time()))

    counter -= 1


threadLock = threading.Lock()

threads = []


# Create new threads

thread1 = myThread(1, "Thread-1", 1)

thread2 = myThread(2, "Thread-2", 2)
```

```
# Start new Threads

thread1.start()

thread2.start()


# Add threads to thread list

threads.append(thread1)

threads.append(thread2)


# Wait for all threads to complete

for t in threads:

    t.join()

print "Exiting Main Thread"
```

When the above code is executed, it produces the following result −

```
Starting Thread-1
Starting Thread-2
Thread-1: Thu Mar 21 09:11:28 2013
Thread-1: Thu Mar 21 09:11:29 2013
Thread-1: Thu Mar 21 09:11:30 2013
Thread-2: Thu Mar 21 09:11:32 2013
Thread-2: Thu Mar 21 09:11:34 2013
Thread-2: Thu Mar 21 09:11:36 2013
Exiting Main Thread
```

Multithreaded Priority Queue:

The *Queue* module allows you to create a new queue object that can hold a specific number of items. There are following methods to control the Queue –

- **get()** – The get() removes and returns an item from the queue.

- **put()** – The put adds item to a queue.

- **qsize()** – The qsize() returns the number of items that are currently in the queue.

- **empty()** – The empty( ) returns True if queue is empty; otherwise, False.

- **full()** – the full() returns True if queue is full; otherwise, False.

Example:

```
#!/usr/bin/python


import Queue

import threading

import time


exitFlag = 0
```

```python
class myThread (threading.Thread):
    def __init__(self, threadID, name, q):
        threading.Thread.__init__(self)
        self.threadID = threadID
        self.name = name
        self.q = q
    def run(self):
        print "Starting " + self.name
        process_data(self.name, self.q)
        print "Exiting " + self.name


def process_data(threadName, q):
    while not exitFlag:
        queueLock.acquire()
        if not workQueue.empty():
            data = q.get()
            queueLock.release()
            print "%s processing %s" % (threadName, data)
```

```
      else:

         queueLock.release()

      time.sleep(1)


threadList = ["Thread-1", "Thread-2", "Thread-3"]

nameList = ["One", "Two", "Three", "Four", "Five"]

queueLock = threading.Lock()

workQueue = Queue.Queue(10)

threads = []

threadID = 1


# Create new threads

for tName in threadList:

   thread = myThread(threadID, tName, workQueue)

   thread.start()

   threads.append(thread)

   threadID += 1


# Fill the queue
```

```
queueLock.acquire()

for word in nameList:

    workQueue.put(word)

queueLock.release()


# Wait for queue to empty

while not workQueue.empty():

    pass


# Notify threads it's time to exit

exitFlag = 1


# Wait for all threads to complete

for t in threads:

    t.join()

print "Exiting Main Thread"
```

When the above code is executed, it produces the following result −

```
Starting Thread-1
Starting Thread-2
```

```
Starting Thread-3
Thread-1 processing One
Thread-2 processing Two
Thread-3 processing Three
Thread-1 processing Four
Thread-2 processing Five
Exiting Thread-3
Exiting Thread-1
Exiting Thread-2
Exiting Main Thread
```

Python - XML Processing

XML is a portable, open source language that allows programmers to develop applications that can be read by other applications, regardless of operating system and/or developmental language.

What is XML?

The Extensible Markup Language (XML) is a markup language much like HTML or SGML. This is recommended by the World Wide Web Consortium and available as an open standard.

XML is extremely useful for keeping track of small to medium amounts of data without requiring a SQL-based backbone.

XML Parser Architectures and APIs

The Python standard library provides a minimal but useful set of interfaces to work with XML.

The two most basic and broadly used APIs to XML data are the SAX and DOM interfaces.

- **Simple API for XML (SAX)** – Here, you register callbacks for events of interest and then let the parser proceed through the document. This is useful when your documents are large or you have memory limitations, it parses the file as it reads it from disk and the entire file is never stored in memory.

- **Document Object Model (DOM) API** – This is a World Wide Web Consortium recommendation wherein the entire file is read into memory and stored in a hierarchical (tree-based) form to represent all the features of an XML document.

SAX obviously cannot process information as fast as DOM can when working with large files. On the other hand, using DOM exclusively can really kill your resources, especially if used on a lot of small files.

SAX is read-only, while DOM allows changes to the XML file. Since these two different APIs literally complement each other, there is no reason why you cannot use them both for large projects.

For all our XML code examples, let's use a simple XML file *movies.xml* as an input –

```
<collection shelf="New Arrivals">
<movie title="Enemy Behind">
  <type>War, Thriller</type>
  <format>DVD</format>
  <year>2003</year>
```

```
   <rating>PG</rating>

   <stars>10</stars>

   <description>Talk about a US-Japan war</description>

</movie>

<movie title="Transformers">

   <type>Anime, Science Fiction</type>

   <format>DVD</format>

   <year>1989</year>

   <rating>R</rating>

   <stars>8</stars>

   <description>A schientific fiction</description>

</movie>

   <movie title="Trigun">

   <type>Anime, Action</type>

   <format>DVD</format>

   <episodes>4</episodes>

   <rating>PG</rating>

   <stars>10</stars>

   <description>Vash the Stampede!</description>
```

```
</movie>

<movie title="Ishtar">

  <type>Comedy</type>

  <format>VHS</format>

  <rating>PG</rating>

  <stars>2</stars>

  <description>Viewable boredom</description>

</movie>

</collection>
```

Parsing XML with SAX APIs:

SAX is a standard interface for event-driven XML parsing. Parsing XML with SAX generally requires you to create your own ContentHandler by subclassing xml.sax.ContentHandler.

Your *ContentHandler* handles the particular tags and attributes of your flavor(s) of XML. A ContentHandler object provides methods to handle various parsing events. Its owning parser calls ContentHandler methods as it parses the XML file.

The methods *startDocument* and *endDocument* are called at the start and the end of the XML file. The method *characters(text)* is passed character data of the XML file via the parameter text.

The ContentHandler is called at the start and end of each element. If the parser is not in namespace mode, the methods *startElement(tag,*
attributes) and *endElement(tag)* are called; otherwise, the corresponding
methods *startElementNS* and *endElementNS* are called. Here, tag is the element tag, and attributes is an Attributes object.

Here are other important methods to understand before proceeding –

The *make_parser* Method:

Following method creates a new parser object and returns it. The parser object created will be of the first parser type the system finds.

```
xml.sax.make_parser( [parser_list] )
```

Here is the detail of the parameters –

- **parser_list** – The optional argument consisting of a list of parsers to use which must all implement the make_parser method.

The *parse* Method:

Following method creates a SAX parser and uses it to parse a document.

```
xml.sax.parse( xmlfile, contenthandler[, errorhandler])
```

Here is the detail of the parameters −

- **xmlfile** − This is the name of the XML file to read from.

- **contenthandler** − This must be a ContentHandler object.

- **errorhandler** − If specified, errorhandler must be a SAX ErrorHandler object.

The *parseString* Method:

There is one more method to create a SAX parser and to parse the specified **XML string**.

```
xml.sax.parseString(xmlstring,                 contenthandler[,
errorhandler])
```

Here is the detail of the parameters −

- **xmlstring** − This is the name of the XML string to read from.

- **contenthandler** − This must be a ContentHandler object.

- **errorhandler** – If specified, errorhandler must be a SAX ErrorHandler object.

Example

```
#!/usr/bin/python

import xml.sax

class MovieHandler( xml.sax.ContentHandler ):
  def __init__(self):
    self.CurrentData = ""
    self.type = ""
    self.format = ""
    self.year = ""
    self.rating = ""
    self.stars = ""
    self.description = ""

  # Call when an element starts
  def startElement(self, tag, attributes):
```

```python
        self.CurrentData = tag

        if tag == "movie":

            print "*****Movie*****"

            title = attributes["title"]

            print "Title:", title


# Call when an elements ends

def endElement(self, tag):

    if self.CurrentData == "type":

        print "Type:", self.type

    elif self.CurrentData == "format":

        print "Format:", self.format

    elif self.CurrentData == "year":

        print "Year:", self.year

    elif self.CurrentData == "rating":

        print "Rating:", self.rating

    elif self.CurrentData == "stars":

        print "Stars:", self.stars

    elif self.CurrentData == "description":
```

```python
        print "Description:", self.description
      self.CurrentData = ""


    # Call when a character is read
    def characters(self, content):
      if self.CurrentData == "type":
        self.type = content
      elif self.CurrentData == "format":
        self.format = content
      elif self.CurrentData == "year":
        self.year = content
      elif self.CurrentData == "rating":
        self.rating = content
      elif self.CurrentData == "stars":
        self.stars = content
      elif self.CurrentData == "description":
        self.description = content

if ( __name__ == "__main__"):
```

```
# create an XMLReader

parser = xml.sax.make_parser()

# turn off namepsaces

parser.setFeature(xml.sax.handler.feature_namespaces, 0)


# override the default ContextHandler

Handler = MovieHandler()

parser.setContentHandler( Handler )


parser.parse("movies.xml")
```

This would produce following result –

```
*****Movie*****
Title: Enemy Behind
Type: War, Thriller
Format: DVD
Year: 2003
Rating: PG
Stars: 10
Description: Talk about a US-Japan war
*****Movie*****
Title: Transformers
Type: Anime, Science Fiction
Format: DVD
```

```
Year: 1989
Rating: R
Stars: 8
Description: A schientific fiction
*****Movie*****
Title: Trigun
Type: Anime, Action
Format: DVD
Rating: PG
Stars: 10
Description: Vash the Stampede!
*****Movie*****
Title: Ishtar
Type: Comedy
Format: VHS
Rating: PG
Stars: 2
Description: Viewable boredom
```

For a complete detail on SAX API documentation, please refer to standard <u>Python SAX APIs</u>.

Parsing XML with DOM APIs:

The Document Object Model ("DOM") is a cross-language API from the World Wide Web Consortium (W3C) for accessing and modifying XML documents.

The DOM is extremely useful for random-access applications. SAX only allows you a view of one bit of the document at a time. If you are looking at one SAX element, you have no access to another.

Here is the easiest way to quickly load an XML document and to create a minidom object using the xml.dom module. The minidom object provides a simple parser method that quickly creates a DOM tree from the XML file.

The sample phrase calls the parse(file [,parser]) function of the minidom object to parse the XML file designated by file into a DOM tree object.

```python
#!/usr/bin/python


from xml.dom.minidom import parse

import xml.dom.minidom


# Open XML document using minidom parser

DOMTree = xml.dom.minidom.parse("movies.xml")

collection = DOMTree.documentElement

if collection.hasAttribute("shelf"):

    print "Root element : %s" % collection.getAttribute("shelf")


# Get all the movies in the collection

movies = collection.getElementsByTagName("movie")
```

```
# Print detail of each movie.

for movie in movies:

  print "*****Movie*****"

  if movie.hasAttribute("title"):

    print "Title: %s" % movie.getAttribute("title")


  type = movie.getElementsByTagName('type')[0]

  print "Type: %s" % type.childNodes[0].data

  format = movie.getElementsByTagName('format')[0]

  print "Format: %s" % format.childNodes[0].data

  rating = movie.getElementsByTagName('rating')[0]

  print "Rating: %s" % rating.childNodes[0].data

  description = movie.getElementsByTagName('description')[0]

  print "Description: %s" % description.childNodes[0].data
```

This would produce the following result −

```
Root element : New Arrivals
*****Movie*****
Title: Enemy Behind
Type: War, Thriller
```

```
Format: DVD
Rating: PG
Description: Talk about a US-Japan war
*****Movie*****
Title: Transformers
Type: Anime, Science Fiction
Format: DVD
Rating: R
Description: A schientific fiction
*****Movie*****
Title: Trigun
Type: Anime, Action
Format: DVD
Rating: PG
Description: Vash the Stampede!
*****Movie*****
Title: Ishtar
Type: Comedy
Format: VHS
Rating: PG
Description: Viewable boredom
```

For a complete detail on DOM API documentation, please refer to standard Python DOM APIs.

Python - GUI Programming

Python provides various options for developing graphical user interfaces (GUIs). Most important are listed below.

- **Tkinter** – Tkinter is the Python interface to the Tk GUI toolkit shipped with Python. We would look this option in this chapter.

- **wxPython** – This is an open-source Python interface for wxWindows http://wxpython.org.

- **JPython** – JPython is a Python port for Java which gives Python scripts seamless access to Java class libraries on the local machine http://www.jython.org.

There are many other interfaces available, which you can find them on the net.

Tkinter Programming:

Tkinter is the standard GUI library for Python. Python when combined with Tkinter provides a fast and easy way to create GUI applications. Tkinter provides a powerful object-oriented interface to the Tk GUI toolkit.

Creating a GUI application using Tkinter is an easy task. All you need to do is perform the following steps –

- Import the *Tkinter* module.

- Create the GUI application main window.

- Add one or more of the above-mentioned widgets to the GUI application.

- Enter the main event loop to take action against each event triggered by the user.

Example:

```
#!/usr/bin/python

import Tkinter
top = Tkinter.Tk()
# Code to add widgets will go here...
top.mainloop()
```

This would create a following window –

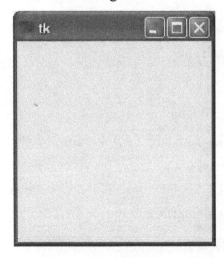

Tkinter Widgets:

Tkinter provides various controls, such as buttons, labels and text boxes used in a GUI application. These controls are commonly called widgets.

There are currently 15 types of widgets in Tkinter. We present these widgets as well as a brief description in the following table –

Sr.No.	Operator & Description
1	**Button** The Button widget is used to display buttons in your application.
2	**Canvas** The Canvas widget is used to draw shapes, such as lines, ovals, polygons and rectangles, in your application.
3	**Checkbutton** The Checkbutton widget is used to display a number of options as checkboxes. The user can select multiple options at a time.

4	**Entry**
	The Entry widget is used to display a single-line text field for accepting values from a user.
5	**Frame**
	The Frame widget is used as a container widget to organize other widgets.
6	**Label**
	The Label widget is used to provide a single-line caption for other widgets. It can also contain images.
7	**Listbox**
	The Listbox widget is used to provide a list of options to a user.
8	**Menubutton**
	The Menubutton widget is used to display menus in your application.
9	**Menu**
	The Menu widget is used to provide various

	commands to a user. These commands are contained inside Menubutton.
10	**Message** The Message widget is used to display multiline text fields for accepting values from a user.
11	**Radiobutton** The Radiobutton widget is used to display a number of options as radio buttons. The user can select only one option at a time.
12	**Scale** The Scale widget is used to provide a slider widget.
13	**Scrollbar** The Scrollbar widget is used to add scrolling capability to various widgets, such as list boxes.
14	**Text** The Text widget is used to display text in multiple lines.

15	**Toplevel**
	The Toplevel widget is used to provide a separate window container.
16	**Spinbox**
	The Spinbox widget is a variant of the standard Tkinter Entry widget, which can be used to select from a fixed number of values.
17	**PanedWindow**
	A PanedWindow is a container widget that may contain any number of panes, arranged horizontally or vertically.
18	**LabelFrame**
	A labelframe is a simple container widget. Its primary purpose is to act as a spacer or container for complex window layouts.
19	**tkMessageBox**
	This module is used to display message boxes in your applications.

Let us study these widgets in detail −

Standard attributes:

Let us take a look at how some of their common attributes.such as sizes, colors and fonts are specified.

- Dimensions

- Colors

- Fonts

- Anchors

- Relief styles

- Bitmaps

- Cursors

Let us study them briefly −

Geometry Management:

All Tkinter widgets have access to specific geometry management methods, which have the purpose of organizing widgets throughout the parent widget area. Tkinter exposes the following geometry manager classes: pack, grid, and place.

- The *pack()* Method − This geometry manager organizes widgets in blocks before placing them in the parent widget.

- The *grid()* Method – This geometry manager organizes widgets in a table-like structure in the parent widget.

- The *place()* Method – This geometry manager organizes widgets by placing them in a specific position in the parent widget.

Python - Extension Programming with C

Any code that you write using any compiled language like C, C++, or Java can be integrated or imported into another Python script. This code is considered as an "extension."

A Python extension module is nothing more than a normal C library. On Unix machines, these libraries usually end in **.so** (for shared object). On Windows machines, you typically see **.dll** (for dynamically linked library).

Pre-Requisites for Writing Extensions

To start writing your extension, you are going to need the Python header files.

- On Unix machines, this usually requires installing a developer-specific package such as python2.5-dev.

- Windows users get these headers as part of the package when they use the binary Python installer.

Additionally, it is assumed that you have good knowledge of C or C++ to write any Python Extension using C programming.

First look at a Python Extension:

For your first look at a Python extension module, you need to group your code into four part –

- The header file *Python.h*.

- The C functions you want to expose as the interface from your module.

- A table mapping the names of your functions as Python developers see them to C functions inside the extension module.

- An initialization function.

The Header File *Python.h*

You need include *Python.h* header file in your C source file, which gives you access to the internal Python API used to hook your module into the interpreter.

Make sure to include Python.h before any other headers you might need. You need to follow the includes with the functions you want to call from Python.

The C Functions:

The signatures of the C implementation of your functions always takes one of the following three forms −

```
static PyObject *MyFunction( PyObject *self, PyObject *args );



static   PyObject   *MyFunctionWithKeywords(PyObject *self,
```

```
                        PyObject *args,

                        PyObject *kw);


static PyObject *MyFunctionWithNoArgs( PyObject *self
);
```

Each one of the preceding declarations returns a Python object. There is no such thing as a *void* function in Python as there is in C. If you do not want your functions to return a value, return the C equivalent of Python's **None** value. The Python headers define a macro, Py_RETURN_NONE, that does this for us.

The names of your C functions can be whatever you like as they are never seen outside of the extension module. They are defined as *static* function.

Your C functions usually are named by combining the Python module and function names together, as shown here −

```
static PyObject *module_func(PyObject *self, PyObject
*args) {

  /* Do your stuff here. */

  Py_RETURN_NONE;

}
```

This is a Python function called *func* inside of the module *module*. You will be putting pointers to your C functions into the method table for the module that usually comes next in your source code.

The Method Mapping Table:

This method table is a simple array of PyMethodDef structures. That structure looks something like this −

```
struct PyMethodDef {

  char *ml_name;

  PyCFunction ml_meth;

  int ml_flags;

  char *ml_doc;

};
```

Here is the description of the members of this structure −

- **ml_name** − This is the name of the function as the Python interpreter presents when it is used in Python programs.

- **ml_meth** − This must be the address to a function that has any one of the signatures described in previous seection.

- **ml_flags** – This tells the interpreter which of the three signatures ml_meth is using.

    o This flag usually has a value of METH_VARARGS.

    o This flag can be bitwise OR'ed with METH_KEYWORDS if you want to allow keyword arguments into your function.

    o This can also have a value of METH_NOARGS that indicates you do not want to accept any arguments.

- **ml_doc** – This is the docstring for the function, which could be NULL if you do not feel like writing one.

This table needs to be terminated with a sentinel that consists of NULL and 0 values for the appropriate members.

Example

For the above-defined function, we have following method mapping table –

```
static PyMethodDef module_methods[] = {

   { "func", (PyCFunction)module_func, METH_NOARGS,
NULL },
```

```
{ NULL, NULL, 0, NULL }

};
```

The Initialization Function

The last part of your extension module is the initialization function. This function is called by the Python interpreter when the module is loaded. It is required that the function be named **init***Module*, where *Module* is the name of the module.

The initialization function needs to be exported from the library you will be building. The Python headers define PyMODINIT_FUNC to include the appropriate incantations for that to happen for the particular environment in which we're compiling. All you have to do is use it when defining the function.

Your C initialization function generally has the following overall structure −

```
PyMODINIT_FUNC initModule() {

  Py_InitModule3(func, module_methods, "docstring...");

}
```

Here is the description of *Py_InitModule3* function −

- **func** – This is the function to be exported.

- *module*_**methods** – This is the mapping table name defined above.

- *docstring* – This is the comment you want to give in your extension.

Putting this all together looks like the following –

```c
#include <Python.h>


static PyObject *module_func(PyObject *self, PyObject *args) {

  /* Do your stuff here. */

  Py_RETURN_NONE;

}


static PyMethodDef module_methods[] = {

  { "func", (PyCFunction)module_func, METH_NOARGS, NULL },

  { NULL, NULL, 0, NULL }

};
```

```
PyMODINIT_FUNC initModule() {

  Py_InitModule3(func, module_methods, "docstring...");

}
```

Example

A simple example that makes use of all the above concepts −

```
#include <Python.h>


static PyObject* helloworld(PyObject* self) {

  return Py_BuildValue("s", "Hello, Python extensions!!");

}


static char helloworld_docs[] =

  "helloworld( ): Any message you want to put here!!\n";


static PyMethodDef helloworld_funcs[] = {

  {"helloworld", (PyCFunction)helloworld,

    METH_NOARGS, helloworld_docs},

    {NULL}
```

```
};


void inithelloworld(void) {

    Py_InitModule3("helloworld", helloworld_funcs,

            "Extension module example!");

}
```

Here the *Py_BuildValue* function is used to build a Python value. Save above code in hello.c file. We would see how to compile and install this module to be called from Python script.

Building and Installing Extensions

The *distutils* package makes it very easy to distribute Python modules, both pure Python and extension modules, in a standard way. Modules are distributed in source form and built and installed via a setup script usually called *setup.py* as follows.

For the above module, you need to prepare following setup.py script –

```
from distutils.core import setup, Extension

setup(name='helloworld', version='1.0', \
```

```
ext_modules=[Extension('helloworld', ['hello.c'])])
```

Now, use the following command, which would perform all needed compilation and linking steps, with the right compiler and linker commands and flags, and copies the resulting dynamic library into an appropriate directory −

```
$ python setup.py install
```

On Unix-based systems, you'll most likely need to run this command as root in order to have permissions to write to the site-packages directory. This usually is not a problem on Windows.

Importing Extensions:

Once you installed your extension, you would be able to import and call that extension in your Python script as follows −

```
#!/usr/bin/python

import helloworld


print helloworld.helloworld()
```

This would produce the following result −

```
Hello, Python extensions!!
```

Passing Function Parameters:

As you will most likely want to define functions that accept arguments, you can use one of the other signatures for your C functions. For example, following function, that accepts some number of parameters, would be defined like this −

```
static PyObject *module_func(PyObject *self, PyObject *args) {

  /* Parse args and do something interesting here. */

  Py_RETURN_NONE;

}
```

The method table containing an entry for the new function would look like this −

```
static PyMethodDef module_methods[] = {

  { "func", (PyCFunction)module_func, METH_NOARGS, NULL },

  { "func", module_func, METH_VARARGS, NULL },

  { NULL, NULL, 0, NULL }

};
```

You can use API *PyArg_ParseTuple* function to extract the arguments from the one PyObject pointer passed into your C function.

The first argument to PyArg_ParseTuple is the args argument. This is the object you will be *parsing*. The second argument is a format string describing the arguments as you expect them to appear. Each argument is represented by one or more characters in the format string as follows.

```c
static PyObject *module_func(PyObject *self, PyObject *args) {
    int i;
    double d;
    char *s;

    if (!PyArg_ParseTuple(args, "ids", &i, &d, &s)) {
        return NULL;
    }

    /* Do something interesting here. */
    Py_RETURN_NONE;
}
```

Compiling the new version of your module and importing it enables you to invoke the new function with any number of arguments of any type –

```
module.func(1, s="three", d=2.0)

module.func(i=1, d=2.0, s="three")

module.func(s="three", d=2.0, i=1)
```

You can probably come up with even more variations.

The *PyArg_ParseTuple* Function

Here is the standard signature for **PyArg_ParseTuple** function –

```
int PyArg_ParseTuple(PyObject* tuple,char* format,...)
```

This function returns 0 for errors, and a value not equal to 0 for success. tuple is the PyObject* that was the C function's second argument. Here *format* is a C string that describes mandatory and optional arguments.

Here is a list of format codes for **PyArg_ParseTuple** function –

Code	C type	Meaning
c	char	A Python string of length 1

		becomes a C char.
d	double	A Python float becomes a C double.
f	float	A Python float becomes a C float.
i	int	A Python int becomes a C int.
l	long	A Python int becomes a C long.
L	long long	A Python int becomes a C long long
O	PyObject*	Gets non-NULL borrowed reference to Python argument.
s	char*	Python string without embedded nulls to C char*.

s#	char*+int	Any Python string to C address and length.
t#	char*+int	Read-only single-segment buffer to C address and length.
u	Py_UNICODE*	Python Unicode without embedded nulls to C.
u#	Py_UNICODE*+int	Any Python Unicode C address and length.
w#	char*+int	Read/write single-segment buffer to C address and length.
z	char*	Like s, also accepts None (sets C char* to NULL).
z#	char*+int	Like s#, also accepts None (sets C char* to NULL).

(...)	as per ...	A Python sequence is treated as one argument per item.
|		The following arguments are optional.
:		Format end, followed by function name for error messages.
;		Format end, followed by entire error message text.

Returning Values:

Py_BuildValue takes in a format string much like *PyArg_ParseTuple* does. Instead of passing in the addresses of the values you are building, you pass in the actual values. Here's an example showing how to implement an add function −

```
static PyObject *foo_add(PyObject *self, PyObject *args)
{
    int a;
```

```c
    int b;

    if (!PyArg_ParseTuple(args, "ii", &a, &b)) {

        return NULL;

    }

    return Py_BuildValue("i", a + b);

}
```

This is what it would look like if implemented in Python –

```python
def add(a, b):
  return (a + b)
```

You can return two values from your function as follows, this would be cauptured using a list in Python.

```c
static    PyObject    *foo_add_subtract(PyObject    *self,
PyObject *args) {

    int a;

    int b;

    if (!PyArg_ParseTuple(args, "ii", &a, &b)) {

        return NULL;

    }
```

```
return Py_BuildValue("ii", a + b, a - b);

}
```

This is what it would look like if implemented in Python –

```
def add_subtract(a, b):
  return (a + b, a - b)
```

The *Py_BuildValue* Function

Here is the standard signature for **Py_BuildValue** function –

```
PyObject* Py_BuildValue(char* format,...)
```

Here *format* is a C string that describes the Python object to build. The following arguments of *Py_BuildValue* are C values from which the result is built. The *PyObject** result is a new reference.

Following table lists the commonly used code strings, of which zero or more are joined into string format.

Code	C type	Meaning
c	char	A C char becomes a Python string of length 1.

d	double	A C double becomes a Python float.
f	float	A C float becomes a Python float.
i	int	A C int becomes a Python int.
l	long	A C long becomes a Python int.
N	PyObject*	Passes a Python object and steals a reference.
O	PyObject*	Passes a Python object and INCREFs it as normal.
O&	convert+void*	Arbitrary conversion
s	char*	C 0-terminated char* to Python string, or NULL to None.

s#	char*+int	C char* and length to Python string, or NULL to None.
u	Py_UNICODE*	C-wide, null-terminated string to Python Unicode, or NULL to None.
u#	Py_UNICODE*+int	C-wide string and length to Python Unicode, or NULL to None.
w#	char*+int	Read/write single-segment buffer to C address and length.
z	char*	Like s, also accepts None (sets C char* to NULL).
z#	char*+int	Like s#, also accepts None (sets C char* to NULL).
(...)	as per ...	Builds Python tuple from C values.

[...]	as per ...	Builds Python list from C values.
{...}	as per ...	Builds Python dictionary from C values, alternating keys and values.

Code {...} builds dictionaries from an even number of C values, alternately keys and values. For example, Py_BuildValue("{issi}",23,"zig","zag",42) returns a dictionary like Python's {23:'zig','zag':42}.

Thank You!